PARCHED NATION: INSIDE PAKISTAN'S DESPERATE BATTLE FOR WATER

A.R Usmani
&
M.A Basit

*"Water shortages present the greatest future threat
to the viability of Pakistan as a state and a society."*

– Anatol Lieven, British author and journalist

Acknowledgment

Special thanks to Aqsa Q. and Zainab J. for their assistance in parts of this book. – A.R. Usmani

Thanks to my mother whose careful use of water at home instilled in me a sense of caring for the precious natural resource. – M.A Basit

About the Authors

A.R. Usmani is an expert wordsmith, linguist, and poet, who has held various leadership roles in the content industry. He holds a degree in Political Science and International Relations from the University of London.

Muhammad A. Basit is a seasoned journalist and columnist with an MPhil in Political Science and a background in Civil Engineering. He specializes in crafting powerful narratives uncovering sociopolitical issues.

Disclaimer

This book is a compilation of research and analysis based on publicly available data, credible reports, and sources cited throughout the text. The views and interpretations presented are the author's personal understanding of the information and are not intended to defame, criticize, or harm any individual, institution, or organization.

The author and publisher do not claim ownership of the facts or statistics cited and are not liable for any errors, omissions, or interpretations arising from the use of this book. Readers are encouraged to verify information independently and approach the content as a starting point for discussion and further exploration.

This book is written in good faith, with the sole aim of contributing to public awareness and fostering constructive dialogue on the water crisis in Pakistan.

Table of Contents

Introduction

Every hour, a child dies in Pakistan from diseases linked to unsafe water. This staggering reality is not just a tragic statistic – it's a harrowing indictment of a system that has failed its people. The question of water – so elemental, so central to human existence – has taken on a profoundly political dimension in Pakistan. For millions, the act of securing water has shifted from routine to uncertain, to now an outright existential struggle.

In urban centers, you will find citizens queue at dawn, clutching empty containers with a faint hope that today will bring relief. In rural areas, women trek miles under a relentless sun, balancing heavy pots of water for their families. These scenes of desperation are not isolated snapshots of poverty but vivid evidence of a system plagued by inequities and crippled by systemic neglect.

In hospitals, grieving parents cradle children dying from waterborne diseases, powerless against the silent killer that flows through contaminated taps. This bleak reality exposes not just a scarcity of resources but a clear failure to prioritize survival over profit and accountability over indifference. Pakistan stands on the brink – a worsening water disaster threatens to bring instability and even a system collapse in the years ahead unless something is done.

In a country that swings between the extremes of floods and droughts, stable access to water remains elusive. The question is not merely why this happens but why it is allowed to persist. Is it climate change? Is it external pressures, such as transboundary water disputes with India?

Or does the answer lie closer to home – in a corrupt and myopic political apparatus that has turned resource management into an instrument of control and profit?

This crisis is not confined to empty taps and dry canals. It has far-reaching consequences that demand a radical shift in how we understand water and governance. The scarcity is not natural; it is manufactured, a predictable outcome of policies that prioritize short-term political gains over long-term public good.

This book uncovers the stories of communities grappling with daily water scarcity, the bureaucratic inertia that exacerbates the problem, and the political dynamics that prevent and, indeed, at times, oppose meaningful change. It also examines the broader implications of this crisis – not just for Pakistan but for the global community. But one question lingers, waiting to be answered: **How does a nation so abundant in water resources end up with the majority of its population desperate for water?**

The issue may not be climate change, or even the oft-cited rival, India. Instead, the heart of Pakistan's water crisis might be buried deep within its governance. Corruption, mismanagement, and a failure to act have left millions without access to this essential resource.

And yet, the question persists – what happens when a country of over 250 million people finally runs out of water? The consequences ripple far beyond its borders, potentially triggering mass migrations, geopolitical tensions, and economic turmoil. The urgency of the situation cannot be overstated, nor can the necessity for immediate, comprehensive action. What will the world do, when faced with a nuclear-armed nation parched and desperate?

Yet, there is not a shortage of hope. The resilience and ingenuity of Pakistan's people may shine through, offering lessons in perseverance and innovation. From grassroots movements advocating for better water management to communities reviving ancient water conservation techniques, there are glimmers of solutions that, if scaled and supported, could turn the tide.

This book is more than a chronicle of Pakistan's water crisis; it is a call to action. It demands that we finally confront uncomfortable truths about the systems that perpetuate scarcity and the ideologies that justify inequality. It invites policymakers, activists, and citizens to rethink water not as a commodity but as a public good, inseparable from the fundamental rights and dignity of people and the country's national security.

The stakes could not be higher. Pakistan's water crisis is a warning – a signal that the global challenges of resource depletion, climate change, and governance cannot be addressed in isolation. What happens when a nation runs dry is not a theoretical question but an imminent reality, one with implications for us all. The time to act is now – not through half-measures or platitudes but through the structural changes necessary to ensure that water, the essence of life, remains accessible to all.

In the chapters that follow, we will explore the intricate web of political, economic, and social factors that have brought Pakistan to this point. But we will also explore the possibilities—the ways in which this crisis might serve as a turning point, an opportunity to rethink not only water but governance, equity, and the priorities of a nation and a global community.

Chapter 1: Ground Realities

In Baldia Town, a densely populated suburb of Karachi, desperation hangs in the air thicker than the acrid smell of the open sewers. A crowd jostles at the water point, squabbling over the three small taps. Each person is eager to fill their blue plastic containers, which line up against a wall bearing a painted but unenforced rule: *"No more than 10 liters per person."*

Among the throng is Nasir, a man in his late sixties with a white beard and a Sindhi topi (cap) perched proudly on his head. The topi is not just headgear; it's a symbol of pride and tradition for the people of Sindh, the province of which Karachi is the capital. Nasir moves with a quiet determination, unfazed by the chaos around him. His mission is singular: to secure enough water for his family for the day.

Just a few meters away, Imran, a weathered man of sixty, unloads his tanks from a rickety trailer. Under the sweltering sun, where temperatures can soar to a blistering 45°C (113°F), Imran makes up to ten trips daily, each time hauling about twenty containers filled with precious water. *"I charge for transportation,"* he explains, *"10 rupees (3.6 US cents) per gallon (4.5 liters). The situation is deteriorating because the population is increasing and the water supply is continuously decreasing."* Imran's meager earnings barely cover his costs, but he perseveres, driven by the knowledge that his neighbors depend on him.

Imran, like many others, transports this poor-quality yet vital drinking water to another part of Baldia Town, where 320,000 residents live without direct access to clean water. *"The biggest injustice,"* he says, frustration etched in his voice, *"is that I am still paying my bills to the Karachi*

Water and Sewerage Board (KWSB) for water that never comes."

In another corner of Karachi lies Orangi Town, a sprawling, unplanned settlement that houses over two million people. Navigating its maze of narrow, winding lanes and broken roads, one finds endless rows of small concrete houses crammed together. Orangi is a city within a city, a testament to numerous hopefuls looking to better their lives in the vast metropolitan. But for all its resourcefulness, Orangi has run dry.

"What water?" asks Sania Begum, a 60-year-old resident. *"We don't get any water here."* The last time water flowed through the main pipeline in her neighborhood was over a month ago, a distant memory that has left residents skeptical of ever seeing water in their taps again.

In a twisted sense, some might consider Orangi's residents "lucky" because they do not rely solely on water tankers, whose availability is unpredictable and whose prices are prohibitive for many. Instead, they have turned to drilling motor-operated wells, locally known as 'bores'. These bores reach deep into the ground to access groundwater, but in Karachi, a coastal city, this water is often salty and unfit for drinking.

Installing a bore well costs approximately $800 – a staggering amount for Orangi's working-class residents, many of whom earn as little as $120 a month. Farzana Bibi, a 40-year-old mother of five, manages her household on roughly $190 a month. *"I'm piling up the dirty clothes, that's how I save money,"* she says with a weary smile. *"We bathe two days a week."*

Farzana's story is echoed throughout Orangi. The water crisis has forced families to adopt extreme measures to conserve every drop. Children forego their baths, and clothes are worn longer between washes. **Cooking, cleaning, and drinking – basic activities taken for granted elsewhere – become daily challenges in a community where water is more precious than gold.**

Farzana's measures to save water are meticulous. She makes sure never to leave the tap running while washing clothes, filling a basin instead. She waits until she has a fortnight's worth of dirty laundry before starting to wash. Every drop of water, she insists, must be accounted for. Despite these efforts, the water tank at her home is almost always dry. *"There is a small amount of water,"* she says. *"I am saving it to drink. When I have money in my hands, I'll get a tanker."*

The struggle for water extends beyond Baldia and Orangi. In Korangi, another part of Karachi, Imran, a 75-year-old man, tended to his small herd of cows and buffaloes on a plot of land behind his cramped four-room house. For sixteen years, this small herd provided his family's livelihood. Four years ago, when the water supply to his area began to falter, Imran had to give up his animals. Today, his household of seventeen people relies entirely on water bought from tankers.

"The people of the water board are the ones who are doing this," he complains, his voice rising in exasperation. *"They are the ones who create the water crisis, and they're the ones who don't provide the water but take the bills. For every job, there is a price. And if you don't have money, you won't get anything done."*

Fizza Ali, a resident of Punjab Colony, shares a similar plight. *"We get water once every fifteen days, for not more than half an hour,"* says the 20-year-old student. The water from the supply line now has a pungent smell, making it unusable. Some residents who used the water faced severe consequences, from skin rashes to stomach illnesses.

Even those from relatively well-off districts are not spared. Irfan Ali, an employee of the Federal Board of Revenue (FBR), has been a resident of the FC Area for over two decades. *"When I first came here in 1992, we used to get water daily, then it reduced to weekly and then monthly. But in the past 10 years, the water has been completely cut off,"* revealed Irfan. He added that a few years ago, new pipelines and connections were installed in the houses, but the issue of water supply never got resolved. Whenever residents complain about the issue, officials say that *"the lineman is not here"* or *"water has not come from the source."*

Efforts to address the water crisis have been sporadic and insufficient. The government has launched various initiatives, from building new dams to improving water distribution networks, but these projects often fall victim to bureaucratic delays, corruption, and political infighting. In the meantime, private water tankers fill the void, creating a parallel, unregulated water economy that exploits the desperation of Karachi's residents.

For the people of Baldia Town, Orangi, Korangi, and Punjab Colony, every day is a battle for survival. Hassan continues to brave the chaos at the water point, determined to secure enough for his family. Imran makes his ten daily trips, each one a lifeline for his neighbors. Farzana, Irfan, Fizza, and countless others stretch every rupee and every drop of water, praying for a day when clean water will once again flow freely through their taps.

Since the commissioning of the Mangla and Tarbela dams in the 1960s and 1970s, Pakistan has not developed any major water storage infrastructure. Consequently, water storage capacity has often receded to less than 30 days against the minimum requirement of 120 days.

Such tales are common in Karachi, a sprawling megalopolis of over 20 million inhabitants – 35 million if you count those living as non-permanent residents. It is the economic heart of the country and its daily water needs amount to 1,200 million gallons. However, it faces a shortage of about 550 million gallons per day, amplified by the obsolescence of facilities and pipelines.

Yet, the situation in Karachi is a microcosm of a broader crisis affecting Pakistan. Over the last few decades, Pakistan has drastically transformed from a water-abundant country to a water-stressed one. Since the commissioning of the Mangla and Tarbela dams in the 1960s and 1970s, Pakistan has not developed any major water storage infrastructure. **Consequently, water storage capacity has often receded to less than 30 days against the minimum requirement of 120 days.**[1]

Coupled this with an explosive population growth and Pakistan's per capita water availability has decreased by more than 80% in the last 70 years.[2] From a high of

---

[1] UNDP. Water Security in Pakistan: Issues and Challenges (Vol. 3, Issue 4).

[2] The Express Tribune. (2023). Critical water shortage.

9

5,260 cubic meters per person in 1951, it dropped to 1,209 cubic meters in 1981, 1,611 cubic meters in 1991, and then to 908 cubic meters in 2016. Water scarcity is a frightening situation in Pakistan, which ranks 14th among the 17 'extremely high-water risk' countries of the world – a list that includes hot and dry countries like Saudi Arabia. Over 80% of the total population in the country faces 'severe water scarcity' for at least one month of the year.[3]

One of the most glaring issues is Pakistan's woeful storage capacity for its river water. With the capacity to store only up to 10% of its yearly river flows, the country lags significantly behind the global average, which stands at around 40%. Pakistan's total water storage capacity is a mere 13 million acre-feet (MAF) out of a potential 140 MAF, reflecting a critical shortfall in the ability to manage and conserve water resources effectively.

The economic ramifications of this storage crisis are profound. Federal Minister for Water Resources Syed Khurshid Ahmad Shah has highlighted a staggering loss of $10 to $15 billion annually due to water wastage, while the country seeks only $2 billion in international aid.

In stark contrast, countries like India, Egypt, and the United States have vastly superior water storage capabilities. India can carry over water for up to 170 days, Egypt has a capacity of 700 days, and the United States boasts an impressive 900 days. Pakistan, however, struggles with a meager 30 days of water carryover capacity. This disparity highlights the country's

---

[3] Pakistan Institute of Development Economics. (2022). *Water crisis in Pakistan: Manifestation, causes and the way forward.* PIDE Knowledge Brief.

vulnerability in the face of climate variability and extreme weather events.[4]

The situation is further exacerbated by the fact that Pakistan's live water storage capacity has actually decreased over the decades. In 1976, the storage capacity was 16.26 MAF, but it has since reduced to 13.68 MAF. This reduction underscores a growing crisis, as the country's ability to store and manage water has deteriorated even as the population and water demands have surged.

The economic ramifications of this storage crisis are profound. Federal Minister for Water Resources Syed Khurshid Ahmad Shah has highlighted a staggering loss of $10 to $15 billion annually due to water wastage, while the country seeks only $2 billion in international aid. This stark contrast reflects a significant disconnect between the financial losses incurred from mismanagement and the aid being pursued. The mismanagement of water resources thus not only threatens the nation's water security but also its economic stability.

The country's dependence on a single river system is extremely risky: the Indus River system accounts for 95.8% of the total renewable water resources of Pakistan. Moreover, the water originating from outside of Pakistan accounts for over three-fourths (78%) of the total water resources, making the country highly vulnerable to external factors.

When a country cannot sustain enough from its surface reservoirs, it turns to the water underground.

---

[4] Dawn. (2021). Pakistan has only 30-day water carryover capacity: Wapda chief.
https://www.dawn.com/news/1652253/pakistan-has-only-30-day-water-carryover-capacity-wapda-chief

However, Pakistan's groundwater resources – the last resort of water supply – are severely overdrawn, mainly to supply water for irrigation. Despite representing only 3% of the global population and contributing just 0.36% to global GDP, Pakistan accounts for 9% of total global groundwater withdrawals, positioning it as the third-largest user.

Therefore, it is not surprising Pakistan also has the world's second most over-stressed underground water reserve. **The strain on groundwater is very disturbing, as over 60% of irrigation, 70% of drinking water, and 100% of the industry in the country depend on it.**

Further compounding the problem is pollution due to a lack of proper waste management. In Pakistan, 60 million people are at risk of exposure to high concentrations of arsenic in groundwater. The popularity of small wells is also causing the groundwater table to recede at a rapid pace. As one local well-digger stated: *"We used to find water 30-40 feet below the ground. Now it's at 200 feet, sometimes even 500 feet."*

The consequences of this crisis are dire. Agricultural productivity is at risk, food security is threatened, and public health is compromised. The frequent clashes over water in Karachi could become common in other cities as well. As water becomes scarcer, the potential for conflict increases, both within communities and between regions.

Efforts to address the water crisis have been sporadic and insufficient. The government has launched various initiatives, from building new dams to improving water distribution networks, but these projects often fall victim to bureaucratic delays, corruption, and political infighting. In the meantime, private water tankers fill the void, creating a parallel, unregulated water economy that exploits the desperation of Pakistan's residents.

The reality is stark: without immediate and effective intervention, Pakistan's water crisis will not just persist but worsen. The consequences of inaction are dire, not just for Karachi, but for cities and towns across the country. The water crisis, if left unaddressed, has the potential to unravel decades of progress, plunging communities into deeper poverty and triggering widespread social unrest.

The next chapter in this narrative of struggle and resilience takes us deeper into the heart of the issue: ***de-development***. As the water crisis intensifies, its ripple effects are felt across all sectors of society, leading to the regression of development. The once-promising strides in infrastructure, healthcare, education, and economic growth are at risk of being undone, pushing Pakistan back to a state of underdevelopment.

Chapter 2: De-Development

The water crisis in Pakistan is not only a tale of scarcity but also one of severe de-development. As the country grapples with dwindling water resources, the lack of clean water and sanitation facilities is reversing decades of progress and pushing communities into a cycle of poverty and illness.

De-development refers to the process by which a country or region experiences a reversal in development, where gains in infrastructure, healthcare, education, and economic stability are undermined or lost. This concept highlights the destructive impact of crises that not only halt progress but actively roll back improvements, leading to a decline in living standards and quality of life.

In the context of Pakistan, de-development is manifested in several distressing ways. The once-promising advances in infrastructure are now compromised by failing water management systems. Healthcare facilities, which had made strides in combating waterborne diseases, are overwhelmed and under-resourced. Educational gains are at risk as children miss school to help their families fetch water or fall ill due to inadequate sanitation. Economic growth is stunted as businesses and agriculture suffer from water shortages, leading to increased poverty and unemployment.

As of now, only 58 percent of the population has access to basic sanitation. This alarming statistic highlights a worsening situation over the decades. Elders often reminisce about a bygone era when they drank tap water without hesitation. In those days, there was no sewage disposal into the rivers, washes, and canals. Canal water, though cool and muddy, was clean. The Nullah Lai in Rawalpindi flowed with clear water, and the washes of the new capital city were pristine. Murree was famous for its 'Chashmas' (natural fountains), and no one had to carry bottled water.

Islamabad, the capital city, was the first to feel the sting of contaminated water. It was discovered that the city's clean and dirty water lines were laid underground in close proximity. Over the years, due to a lack of maintenance, these lines mixed, leading to an epidemic of hepatitis. The once-safe water turned hazardous, marking the beginning of a nationwide crisis.

The situation further deteriorated when sewage treatment plants became non-functional. The sewage plant at Mahmood Booti in Lahore stopped working, allowing the city's dirty water to flow into the already water-starved Ravi River due to the Indus Water Treaty. Downstream communities, consuming this contaminated water, experienced a widespread hepatitis epidemic. What began in Islamabad spread across the country through the interconnected waterways, transforming nature's gift into a source of disease and death.

Pakistan ranks 80th out of 122 countries for drinking water availability, a dire ranking for a nation of its size and rapidly growing population. From 1951 to the present, the population has surged from 34 million to 250 million. **Of this, 80 percent are forced to drink contaminated water.** Studies from sampled areas, extrapolated to the rest of the country, reveal that except for some places where contamination is low to medium, most of Pakistan suffers from a severe shortage of clean drinking water.[5]

The de-development resulting from this crisis is multifaceted. In rural areas, agricultural productivity is severely impacted. Farmers struggle to irrigate their crops with the limited and often contaminated water available, leading to reduced yields and economic instability. This, in turn, threatens food security for millions, pushing families deeper into poverty. The rural exodus to urban areas exacerbates the already strained resources in cities like Karachi, where the infrastructure is unable to cope with the influx of people seeking better living conditions.

Urban areas are not spared either. The lack of clean water and sanitation in densely populated cities results in the spread of waterborne diseases. Hospitals are overwhelmed with cases of hepatitis, cholera, and dysentery. Public health systems, already under strain, are pushed to their limits, diverting resources that could have been used for other developmental purposes. The economic cost of treating these diseases is enormous, further burdening an already struggling economy.

The water crisis also stifles industrial growth. Factories require a reliable supply of clean water for their operations. The scarcity and contamination of water disrupt production processes, leading to economic losses and hindering the country's industrial development. Foreign

---

[5] Ishaque, W., Sultan, K., & Zia ur Rehman, Z. Water management and sustainable development in Pakistan: Environmental and health impacts of water quality on achieving the UNSDGs by 2030. Frontiers.https://www.frontiersin.org/journals/water/articles/10.3389/fr wa.2024.1267164/full

investors are deterred by the unreliable water supply, further limiting economic opportunities.

Pollution exacerbates the problem. Poor waste management practices lead to the contamination of water sources with industrial effluents and agricultural runoff. In Pakistan, 60 million people are at risk of exposure to high concentrations of arsenic in groundwater. This toxic pollution, combined with the over-extraction of groundwater, is causing the water table to recede at an alarming rate. Wells that once provided water at 30-40 feet below the ground now need to be dug as deep as 200-500 feet, making water access even more challenging and costly.

At any given time, a significant percentage of people in Pakistan are suffering from one or more diseases associated with inadequate drinking water and sanitation. Many rely on the burgeoning filtration business for drinking water, setting up small RO (reverse osmosis) water plants inside their shops or homes to supply filtered water to households. Although RO plants may provide water that is safer to drink compared to piped water, it is still not entirely safe. *"Most of these RO plants do not follow the required environmental health cleaning sanitization requirements,"* says a local health official.

In rural areas, the situation is even more dire. People rely on deep underground aquifers for fresh water. The rural areas of Sindh and southern Punjab depend on these deep wells for drinking and other water uses, but they are gradually drying up. As these traditional sources become less reliable, people are turning to alternative sources of water that are fraught with health hazards. The warmest province of Pakistan, Sindh, faces massive heat waves, particularly from May to September each year, increasing the demand for drinking water. Due to the lack of potable water, people are frequently dehydrated, leading to organ failure and kidney-related issues.

The combined effects of water scarcity and pollution contribute to the spread of diseases. Even the few areas seemingly privileged with clean water are not immune to the effect of contamination. Ans Mujahid, a seasoned horticulturist from southern Punjab is all too aware of the containments that eventually find their way into households through the food they eat. When we spoke to him, he highlighted concerns about observing the extensive use of untreated wastewater and sewage for irrigation due to water scarcity.

"This has led to soil contamination and the uptake of harmful compounds in edible crops, posing serious health risks. Despite a ban on this practice, farmers are still drawn to using wastewater due to the lack of water charges and its nutrient content as fertilizer. Approximately 25% of the vegetables consumed in the country are irrigated with wastewater, and numerous mango orchards in southern Punjab are fertigated using sewage," Ans told us.

Beyond the human toll, the economic impact is staggering. The World Bank warns that Pakistan's GDP could plummet by 18 to 20 percent annually by 2050 if the water crisis remains unaddressed.

The de-development caused by the water crisis in Pakistan is a complex and urgent issue. It affects every aspect of life, from health and education to agriculture and industry. Without immediate and comprehensive action, the situation will continue to deteriorate, pushing the country further into a state of regression.

Pakistan's water crisis is not just an environmental disaster; it is an economic catastrophe as well. The scarcity and contamination of water are not merely inconveniences but profound barriers to the nation's development.

Making people sick, these water-borne illnesses fill about one-third of hospital beds and cause 40 percent of all premature deaths in the country. Beyond the human toll, the economic impact is staggering. The World Bank warns that Pakistan's GDP could plummet by 18 to 20 percent annually by 2050 if the water crisis remains unaddressed.[6]

The education sector, too, is reeling from the water crisis. In many parts of Pakistan, schools lack basic sanitation facilities, forcing students, especially girls, to miss classes. The dropout rate increases as children fall sick due to contaminated water or are needed at home to help with the arduous task of fetching water.

This is true especially in rural schools of Sindh and Balochistan. Children are forced to miss classes to fetch water. Girls are disproportionately affected, often dropping out entirely as families prioritize their labor over their education. A UNESCO report states that the dropout rate for girls in water-scarce areas is nearly double that of boys. The long-term impact on gender equality and economic growth is profound.[7]

---

[6] World Bank. (2022). Pakistan urgently needs significant investments in climate resilience to secure its economy and reduce poverty

[7] UNESCO. (2024). Water crises threaten world peace.

Overall, this lack of education perpetuates the cycle of poverty and underdevelopment, as the next generation is deprived of the skills and knowledge needed to improve their circumstances.

Healthcare systems are overwhelmed by the influx of patients suffering from waterborne diseases. In cities like Karachi and Lahore, hospitals are often at full capacity, with patients suffering from hepatitis, cholera, anemia, and dysentery.

The financial burden on the healthcare system is immense, diverting resources from other critical health initiatives. According to the Pakistan Medical Association, treating waterborne diseases costs the healthcare system billions of rupees annually.[8] This financial strain inhibits the country's ability to invest in other crucial areas of public health.

The agricultural sector, which employs nearly half of Pakistan's workforce, is crippled by water shortages. Farmers in the fertile plains of Punjab and Sindh are facing reduced crop yields due to insufficient irrigation. This not only affects food security but also the livelihoods of millions of farmers. The Indus River, Pakistan's lifeline, is drying up, and with it, the hopes of countless farming communities.

We talked to a climate journalist Muhammad Daud Khan. He covers the environment and climate crisis in Khyber Pakhtunkhwa. He says, *"Every time I meet*

---

[8] Qamar, K., et al. (2022). Water sanitation problem in Pakistan: A review on disease prevalence, strategies for treatment and prevention. Annals of Medicine and Surgery (London),

farmers, they tell me a different story. The farmers are worried about farming in the valley. They are worried about their future because in Kurram, majority of the people are associated with farming".

When farmers look for water, they see their future collapsing in front of their eyes. *"Water is a major challenge in Parachinar Valley. People are buying water containers for drinking. Most of the agricultural land is arid and associated with rain. Sometimes the valley receives rain but most of the time, it remains dry. For the water shortage issue, there is no policy,"* Daud adds.

A recent study by the Pakistan Agricultural Research Council found that water scarcity could reduce agricultural output by up to 40 percent in the next decade.

Osama Rizvi, an economic and energy analyst at Primary Vision Network and Director of Rizvi Insights, weighed in on the situation.

"In terms of food security, the growing population is pushing the need for higher agricultural yields," Rizvi explains. *"We need to increase crop yields to 4.2 percent annually to keep up, but we're currently stagnating at 2.3 percent."* Farmers themselves are not optimistic, pointing out that recent measures have not borne any fruit yet.

He also highlighted another challenge: the rising oil imports. *"Oil import costs are increasing and will continue to do so. This will force the government to choose between importing more oil or securing enough food for the populace."*

The dilemma between fueling the economy and feeding the population could create an even greater strain on Pakistan's resources.

Industries, too, are suffering. Factories require a steady supply of water for their operations. In cities like Faisalabad, known as the *Manchester of Pakistan* for its textile industry, production has slowed down due to water shortages. This impacts not only the local economy but also the national economy, as textiles are a significant export product. The lack of reliable water supply deters foreign investment, further stymying economic growth. The Federation of Pakistan Chambers of Commerce and Industry (FPCCI) estimates that industrial output could fall by 30 percent if the water crisis persists.

The informal economy is also hit hard. Small businesses, which form the backbone of Pakistan's economy, are struggling to survive. Street vendors, small shop owners, and local craftsmen all rely on water for their daily operations. As water becomes more expensive and scarcer, these businesses face closure, leading to increased unemployment and poverty.

In the bustling streets of Lahore, such is the story of Kamal who runs a small bakery. Each morning, he would rise before dawn to knead dough and prepare pastries for his loyal customers. But as the water shortages worsened, Kamal found himself rationing his water supply, leading to inconsistent product quality and rising costs. As water became increasingly scarce and expensive, his once-thriving bakery struggled to stay afloat, leaving him and his employees facing an uncertain future. *"We used to serve hundreds of customers every day,"* Kamal lamented. *"Now, with water so scarce and costly, I'm just trying to keep the lights on and the doors open."*

A survey conducted by the Small and Medium Enterprises Development Authority (SMEDA) revealed that nearly 70 percent of small businesses reported significant losses due to water shortages.

Urban areas are witnessing an alarming rise in water privatization. In the absence of a reliable public water supply, private companies and individuals are stepping in to fill the gap, often at exorbitant prices. This has created a water black market, where only the wealthy can afford clean water. This privatization exacerbates social inequalities, leaving the poor to rely on contaminated sources. A report by the Karachi Water and Sewerage Board (KWSB) found that water prices in some areas had increased by over 200 percent in the past five years.

The environmental impact of Pakistan's water crisis is equally devastating. Once vibrant wetlands, crucial for biodiversity, are now drying up. This loss extends beyond wildlife; local communities that rely on these ecosystems for their livelihoods are also suffering. The Indus Delta, a UNESCO World Heritage site, is shrinking, and with it, the mangrove forests that serve as natural barriers against coastal erosion and provide habitats for numerous species. According to the World Wide Fund for Nature (WWF), Pakistan has lost nearly 90 percent of its mangrove forests in the last 50 years, a sobering indicator of the environmental toll.

The water crisis has also entrenched the country in a cycle of economic stagnation, commonly referred to as stagflation – where slow growth and high inflation coexist, trapping the economy. Pakistan imports more than it exports, straining its foreign reserves. A key solution to this would be attracting more foreign direct investment (FDI). However, as Osama Rizvi highlights during our conversation with him, many investors remain hesitant. *"They foresee worsening conditions due to the lack of focus and political will on the water crisis, which has a direct connection to social stability. Without a concerted effort to address these water-related challenges, the country risks deepening its economic and social struggles,"* Rizvi tells us.

Pakistan stands at a critical juncture where its future development hinges on the urgent resolution of its water crisis. If immediate and decisive action is not taken, the country faces an escalating public health disaster, economic decline, and worsening social inequalities. The grim reality is that failure to address this crisis will not only stymie progress but could lead to a profound de-development, with long-lasting consequences that may be nearly impossible to reverse. Or else, Pakistan must brace itself for a future marred by relentless instability, where the dreams of prosperity and advancement remain forever out of reach. The time to act is now, for the sake of the future of this country, which may not even exist if no concrete actions are taken.

Chapter 3: Water and Gender

In the previous chapter, we explored how Pakistan's water crisis has led to a profound de-development, jeopardizing advances in infrastructure, healthcare, education, and economic growth.

It must also be emphasized that this regression is not felt equally by all; instead, it reveals a deeper, more intimate struggle for those most affected. In the face of dwindling resources, it is crucial to also address the gendered dimension of this crisis that disproportionately burdens women.

Imagine the daily life of Ayesha, a 12-year-old girl living in a small village in rural Pakistan. Each morning, while the sun is still low in the sky, Ayesha wakes up to a day that revolves around one critical task: fetching water. Her routine is dictated by the scarcity of this vital resource. She walks for over three miles to reach the nearest well, carrying an empty container that can hold only a limited amount of water. The trek is arduous, often taking her over two hours just to fill her container, which weighs heavily on her small frame.

Upon her return, Ayesha still has to tend to her household chores and assist her family with daily tasks. The burden of fetching water leaves her with little time or energy to attend school. Education, for her, becomes a distant dream overshadowed by the daily struggle for survival. Her lack of access to water directly impacts her opportunities for learning, limiting her future prospects and perpetuating a cycle of poverty and disenfranchisement.

Water scarcity in Pakistan is a glaring example of how deeply gendered such crises can be. In a country where water is becoming an increasingly precious commodity, the burden of this scarcity falls disproportionately on women. The intersection of water scarcity and gender exposes deep-rooted inequalities and highlights how water issues are intricately linked to broader social and gender norms.

In Pakistan, where water scarcity has reached alarming levels, the responsibility for water collection predominantly rests on women. Studies show that 72% of household water collection in Pakistan is carried out by women, especially in rural areas, informal settlements, and underprivileged localities. Water collection, which should be a fundamental right rather than a burden, impacts women's lives in profound and multifaceted ways.

For many women, collecting water is not just a daily chore but a matter of survival. They face a grim choice each day: risk their lives to fetch water or face the dire consequences of dehydration. In rural areas such as the Tharparkar Desert and the remote regions of Punjab, women undertake arduous journeys that can last up to four hours, carrying heavy clay pots. These trips are not only physically taxing but also mentally draining, with severe implications for their overall well-being.

In this grim reality, the home is no longer a sanctuary but a battleground. At home, women face additional pressures. The lack of sufficient water can lead to intimate partner violence, as families struggle with the frustration and stress of inadequate resources.

The risks associated with these water-fetching expeditions are particularly alarming. Women in these areas often face sexual and physical assault during their long treks. The harsh reality of their situation was starkly highlighted in a report by Human Rights Watch, which detailed numerous incidents of violence against women collecting water in Tharparkar. This violence, coupled with the physical strain of the journey, severely impacts their mental health and safety.

Young girls, who are also tasked with collecting water, face significant barriers to their education. The responsibility of fetching water often takes precedence over attending school, resulting in missed educational opportunities. According to a study by the United Nations Educational, Scientific and Cultural Organization (UNESCO), girls in water-scarce regions are 1.5 times more likely to drop out of school compared to their male counterparts. This educational disadvantage perpetuates the cycle of poverty and limits future opportunities for these girls.

In this grim reality, the home is no longer a sanctuary but a battleground. At home, women face additional pressures. The lack of sufficient water can lead to intimate partner violence, as families struggle with the frustration and stress of inadequate resources.

In regions plagued by severe water shortages, domestic violence spikes as families grapple with the intense stress and frustration of inadequate resources. The lack of water transforms households into pressure cookers where conflicts simmer and sometimes erupt into abuse. As water becomes more precious, the space meant to be a haven turns into a site of strife.

The situation is further compounded in the most remote areas, where **the concept of "Water Wives" has emerged as a grim solution to the water crisis.** In these communities, polygamy is sometimes seen as a practical response to the need for more labor to collect water. Women, burdened by the physical and emotional toll of water collection, may even advocate for their husbands to take additional wives to share the workload.

This phenomenon starkly illustrates how crises can bend social norms to breaking points. Women in these areas often spend their days hauling water, leaving them little time or energy for education or economic opportunities. The practice of "Water Wives" is a desperate measure that reflects the depth of the crisis. It's a tragic reminder of how scarcity not only strips away basic needs but also reshapes social structures in profoundly unsettling ways.

The impact of water scarcity extends beyond individual households and communities. In rural areas where men migrate to urban centers in search of work due to droughts and water shortages, women are left to manage households under increasingly difficult conditions. The absence of male family members not only places an additional burden on women but also heightens their vulnerability to sexual violence and exploitation. This situation is exacerbated by the lack of adequate security and support systems in water-scarce regions.

Mental health issues among women in these areas are particularly troubling. Fieldwork in districts like Tharparkar and Muzaffargarh reveals a concerning trend: women experiencing severe mental stress due to water scarcity and the accompanying migration of men. The high suicide rates in Tharparkar have been linked to the mental health impacts of water scarcity, with isolation and despair contributing to this tragic phenomenon. Women left behind, while their male relatives seek livelihoods elsewhere, face not only the physical challenges of water collection but also profound emotional and psychological distress.

Moreover, the quota system, while intended to increase women's representation, sometimes places individuals in positions of power who are more aligned with political elites than with grassroots realities.

The lack of adequate attention to gender issues in water management and policy further exacerbates these challenges. Despite the critical role women play in managing and collecting water, they are often sidelined in decision-making processes. In Pakistan, women hold less than six percent of federal ministerial positions related to environment, natural resources, and energy.

The situation at the provincial level mirrors this disparity. Women hold only about 14 percent of seats in provincial assemblies. Even within these roles, many are appointed through quotas rather than based on merit. This results in representatives who are disconnected from the realities faced by rural women.

Moreover, the quota system, while intended to increase women's representation, sometimes places individuals in positions of power who are more aligned with political elites than with grassroots realities. This disconnect further alienates rural women, who are left out of discussions and decisions that directly impact their lives.

This underrepresentation has tangible consequences. A study by the World Bank highlights that projects led by women or with significant female involvement tend to have higher success rates in addressing community needs. Yet, with such limited female representation in decision-making roles in Pakistan, the design and implementation of water management solutions often fail to incorporate the insights and needs of the very individuals who are most affected by these issues.

Gendered issues related to water scarcity are not just a matter of individual hardship but a significant barrier to broader socio-economic development. The burden of water collection and the associated risks constrain women's ability to participate fully in economic, educational, and social activities. Addressing these issues is crucial not only for improving women's lives but also for fostering equitable development and progress in Pakistan.

The gendered impact of water scarcity in Pakistan is profound and multifaceted. Women bear the brunt of the water crisis, facing physical dangers, mental stress, and social inequalities as they strive to secure water for their families. The broader implications for education, economic participation, and social stability highlight the urgent need for gender-sensitive approaches to water management and policy.

These dire circumstances underscore a fundamental truth: water scarcity is not just a logistical issue; it is a deeply entrenched social crisis. The daily struggle for water reveals how intertwined resource scarcity is with gender inequality. The lack of access to water doesn't just limit women's physical health and security - it erodes their opportunities, their dignity, and ultimately their status in society.

Without acknowledging these gendered dimensions, Pakistan cannot hope to achieve sustainable development or ensure a fair and just future for all its citizens.

Chapter 4: The Mafia State

Never let a good crisis go to waste. This adage rings disturbingly true in Karachi, Pakistan's financial and commercial capital, where the severe water shortage has given rise to an underground market thriving on the illegal diversion of the city's fire hydrants. Millions of residents, rich and poor alike, have become reliant on this illicit service to meet their daily water needs.

The water crisis in Karachi is severe. **Residents often pay for 72 hours of water supply per week but receive a mere 18 hours.** Officials attribute the shortage to insufficient water availability, but the reality is far more insidious. Much of the city's water is diverted and sold by the so-called "water mafia" – a shadowy network with deep connections to political figures and the police. This illicit trade is an open secret, with those meant to control the theft often being the ones who benefit the most.

The financial implications of this underground market are staggering. By the end of the year, stealing water in Karachi is an industry worth more than half a billion dollars.

Karachi's main pumping station at Dhabeji is supposed to supply the city with 550 million gallons of water per day (MGD). However, this water rarely reaches the intended consumers. **A staggering 42 percent of the water – approximately 235 MGD – is either lost or stolen before it can be distributed.** If the full 550 MGD reached the city, the water supply situation would be manageable, and everyone could have access to this vital resource. Instead, the bulk of Karachi's 'lost' water is stolen and sold back to the very people it was initially meant for.

Water tankers have become an entrenched part of Karachi's water supply landscape over the decades. Initially introduced as a temporary measure while the Karachi Water and Sewerage Board (KWSB) expanded the city's water infrastructure, these tankers have now come to dominate the sector. The government-sanctioned hydrants are tampered with to allow private tanker services to extract and sell far more water than is documented. This tampering occurs at six official hydrants, where flow meters are manipulated to underreport the amount of water extracted. Additionally, two other hydrants, which are not auctioned to private companies, operate with even less accountability.

Beyond these eight official sites, Karachi is dotted with illegal hydrants operated by mafias who siphon water directly from the KWSB mains. The scale of this undocumented water-selling business is so vast that even thorough investigations can barely scratch the surface. According to some reports, there are more than a hundred illegal hydrants, and new ones are constantly being established. These operations are run by individuals with connections in the government, the KWSB, the police, or the revenue department, ensuring their activities continue unimpeded.

Occasionally, public pressure mounts, leading to crackdowns on illegal hydrants. However, these efforts are often superficial. Authorities may demolish a small part of the infrastructure used for theft, but within days, the operations resume as if nothing happened. This cyclical pattern of minimal enforcement followed by quick recovery perpetuates the water mafia's grip on the city's water supply.

The financial implications of this underground market are staggering. If tankers in Karachi make 50,000 trips a day, with each trip priced at an average of Rs 3,000 (prices vary between Rs 1,200 to Rs 7,000), the industry generates approximately Rs 150,000,000 daily. This colossal sum highlights the lucrative nature of the water mafia's operations and the entrenched corruption that sustains it.

That's $1.43 million, every day. In a month, that adds up to $42.3 million. By the end of the year, stealing water in Karachi is an industry worth more than half a billion dollars.

The involvement of political figures and law enforcement in these illegal activities complicates efforts to address the crisis. The people who should be safeguarding Karachi's water supply are instead profiting from its theft. This corruption not only exacerbates the water shortage but also undermines public trust in government institutions.

The water mafia's influence extends beyond the immediate theft and resale of water. Their operations have broader social and economic implications. As the water crisis deepens, the cost of buying water from tankers becomes a significant burden for the city's poorest residents. **Many families are forced to choose between purchasing water and meeting other basic needs, such as food, education, and healthcare.** This financial strain exacerbates inequality in Karachi, pushing the most vulnerable further into hardship and trapping them into a neverending cycle of poverty.

Moreover, the water mafia's dominance stifles efforts to develop sustainable water management solutions. With so much money to be made from the illegal water trade, there is little incentive for those in power to invest in long-term infrastructure improvements. This short-sighted approach leaves Karachi perpetually on the brink of a water catastrophe, with no end in sight.

A similar story unfolds in most other water-parched cities of Pakistan. The social contract, regarding what is the role of the state vis-a-vis the people, is now mediated through the medium of money and privatization. The rights-based approach to water, where water is considered a fundamental right of the people and a fundamental responsibility of the state, has ended. State institutions, rather than working for the benefit of the people, are instead utilized to loot them. Pakistan is a country where people can become billionaires after seizing power. **If the very people responsible for shutting down the illegal theft of water are the ones benefitting from it, who will watch the watchmen?**

While in the south the tanker mafia robs water and sells it at a premium, in the north, Pakistan's fragile system of headwaters is being disrupted by the timber mafia. Trees act as water reservoirs, taking in water from the soil and releasing it through their leaves. The added moisture in the air results in cloud formation, leading to rainfall and the continuation of the water cycle. In Pakistan, as more and more trees are cut down, evaporation levels are disrupted, drying up the moisture in the air and throwing off the balance of the water cycle.

Without trees, there is nothing to hold the soil cover. Soil erosion rates increase, causing concerns of flooding and a higher likelihood of pollutants sweeping into nearby water reservoirs. Monsoon rains and resultant floods throughout Pakistan are one of the main sources of natural contamination. This occurs in concert with the neglect and destruction of sanitation and sewage systems in urban areas and water reservoirs in rural areas.

Like the tanker mafia, timber gangs operate freely in many parts of the country, profiting from illegal logging often with the backing of local officials, neither realizing that their actions are ultimately dooming the nation they and their families live in. Nestled on the west side of Pakistan's Indus River, the remote town of Chilas is notorious for its timber smugglers, who operate freely in the northern district of Gilgit-Baltistan. Chilas is now grappling with the consequences of large swathes of denuded forest. It is experiencing warmer summers and winters, fewer rainy days, frequent landslides, a rise in pest attacks on crops, and a decline in the bird population.

Pakistan has one of the highest deforestation rates in Asia, according to the U.N. Food and Agriculture Organization. Each of Pakistan's five provinces has its own forest laws, intended to regulate forest conservation and timber harvesting according to local needs. But these are routinely ignored, often with the connivance of rural politicians, some of whom encourage their constituents to clear forests, sell the wood, and turn the land into profitable plots for farming or construction.

"Tackling a handful of timber mafia is not really a daunting task. But if these politicians are themselves the timber mafia, how can they wage a war against themselves?" Nazakat Ali, a prominent environmental journalist says.

Clearly, the crises surrounding water and timber in Pakistan reveal a deeply entrenched culture of corruption and exploitation, where public resources are hijacked for private gain. The water and timber mafias, with their extensive networks and political connections, continue to undermine the nation's environmental and public health. These shadowy networks operate with impunity, driven by a relentless pursuit of profit at the expense of the country's natural wealth and the well-being of its people.

The pervasive influence of these groups stifles meaningful reform and perpetuates a cycle of degradation and inequality. The failure to address these issues head-on allows the exploitation of resources to continue unabated, leaving communities to suffer the consequences of unchecked greed. The water crisis, compounded by unchecked deforestation and illegal logging, exemplifies the broader malaise of a system that prioritizes short-term gains over long-term sustainability and justice.

In this context, the need for genuine reform becomes increasingly urgent. However, the path to change is obstructed by a complex web of vested interests and deep pockets. This situation renders efforts to rectify these pressing issues often superficial or ineffective. The result is a grim scenario where the degradation of natural resources and the erosion of public trust continue unabated, casting a long shadow over Pakistan's future.

Without a decisive and coordinated effort to dismantle the networks of corruption and enforce accountability, the country's natural resources and the well-being of its citizens will remain precariously vulnerable. The degradation of Pakistan's environmental and social fabric underscores a broader malaise, where the prospects for meaningful progress are consistently thwarted by those who benefit from maintaining the status quo. Indeed, the survival of future generations hinges on the ability to confront and overcome these entrenched hindrances.

Chapter 5: Political Apathy

As Pakistan faces an unprecedented water crisis, the response from its political leadership has been alarmingly apathetic. As Dr. Ishrat Hussain, an economist and former dean of the Institute of Business Administration, puts it: *"We do not have a water crisis; we have a failure of governance with regard to water issues."*

In any other country facing similar challenges, addressing water scarcity would be a national priority. However, Pakistan's political leadership not only neglects this critical issue but seems to be exacerbating it. The lack of a coherent water policy and the negligence of the authorities are pushing the nation towards a dire future.

The political landscape in Pakistan reflects an attitude of "absentee landlordism" towards water resources. This term aptly describes policymakers who act as if they have no stake or responsibility in managing the country's water crisis. The United Nations Development Programme (UNDP) has highlighted that Pakistani authorities are alarmingly negligent about the worsening water crisis, posing a serious threat to the country's stability. Despite the urgency, the issue is seldom discussed in the national and international media or by policymakers.

The concept of water as a public resource has been eroded, becoming more akin to the private property of landlords, depriving the poor of their fair share. This inequity is further exacerbated by the political elites' unwillingness to disrupt the status quo. The Pakistan Council of Research in Water Resources (PCRWR) warned that the country might run dry by 2025 if immediate actions are not taken. However, instead of taking proactive measures, the political leadership continues business as usual, showing little concern for the impending catastrophe.

Within agriculture, over 80 percent of the country's water resources are used by four major crops: wheat, rice, sugarcane and cotton. These crops contribute only 5 percent to the GDP, highlighting a severe misallocation of resources.

A significant factor contributing to the water crisis is the unsustainable agricultural practices prevalent in the country. Politically powerful feudal lords resist any changes that might reduce their profits, even if such changes are essential for sustainable water management. These feudal lords benefit from heavy subsidies on water usage, further promoting wastage. Canal water, for instance, is immensely underpriced. Only 20 percent of the annual operating and maintenance costs are recovered through abiana (canal water charges), and even then, only 60 percent of total receivables are collected. This system of underpricing and poor collection efficiency leads to a tremendous waste of water resources.

Pakistan extracts 74.3 percent of its freshwater annually, exerting immense pressure on its renewable water resources. **Agriculture remains the largest consumer of water, accounting for 95 percent of annual water withdrawals.** This is followed by industry (including power generation) at 3 percent, and households at a mere 2 percent. Within agriculture, over 80 percent of the country's water resources are used by four major crops: wheat, rice, sugarcane, and cotton. These crops contribute only 5 percent to the GDP, highlighting a severe misallocation of resources. Moreover, three of these four crops (rice, sugarcane, and cotton) have high water usage, an illogical choice for a country where 70 percent of the land is arid to semi-arid.[9]

The political apathy towards the water crisis is further illustrated by the lack of effective water governance. Institutions responsible for water management are either weak or dysfunctional, often mired in corruption and inefficiency. This lack of governance results in poor planning and mismanagement of water resources, exacerbating the crisis. The absence of integrated water resource management, inadequate infrastructure, and insufficient investment in water conservation technologies are clear indicators of the government's failure to address the crisis. One of the most glaring examples of political neglect is the fixation on building huge dams and reservoirs.

Ambreen Shabbir, a transboundary water and policy researcher and independent consultant, shares her thoughts with us: *"A major myth in Pakistan is that the country direly needs reservoir storage. We should realize that reservoirs are not the panacea, at least in the current situation. We are among the countries facing the worst case of climate change impact. Weather variations and climate variability is a pressing concern. In the coming years, rain patterns are going to change drastically. Places with heavy rainfall may turn arid in the next five-ten years while those with scanty rains may start having ample precipitation. Where would we build the reservoirs in this uncertain situation? Imagine spending billions of rupees on a storage*

---

[9] UNDP. Water Security in Pakistan: Issues and Challenges (Vol. 3, Issue 4).

*structure in an area and then having little to no water to
store in it. It by no means implies that dams should not be
built at all. Just be mindful of them."*

These projects are often hailed as silver bullets that
would magically end all water woes in the country. In
reality, simply building new dams isn't the solution when
water distribution and effective management of existing
reservoirs are the bigger issues. Even with such ambitious
plans, political wrangling and bureaucratic inefficiency
have stalled progress. The construction of the Diamer-
Bhasha Dam, for instance, has been delayed for decades
due to political and financial hurdles. *"There isn't any
controversy between provinces on this dam like some
others, yet it does not seem to get into action for decades to
come."* Naseer Memon, a development professional and
columnist at Dawn, shares his thoughts with us while
talking about the lack of political will in addressing the
water challenges at the higher levels.

Misguided priorities and chronic inaction reflect a
broader pattern of neglect and mismanagement that has
long characterized Pakistan's approach to its water
resources. Furthermore, the political leadership's focus on
short-term gains over long-term sustainability has led to
policies that prioritize immediate profits over the future
well-being of the country.

This trend has been all too obvious to Ambreen in
agriculture as well. *"[Pakistan's] cash crops are also the
most water-intensive crops. Our staple food is also a water-
intensive crop. We need to transition in terms of both
domestic and export practices. While transforming
domestic consumption would be challenging and quite*

slow, export transition can be relatively easier," she
shared.

The preference for water-intensive cash crops over
more sustainable agricultural practices is driven by the
desire for quick economic returns. This short-sighted
approach not only depletes water resources but also
undermines the country's food security and economic
stability in the long run.

The water footprint for cotton is alarmingly high:
around 9,800 liters per kilogram. Given that a kilogram of
cotton sells for about $0.71 in the international market,
Pakistan is effectively expending vast quantities of fresh
water for an inconsequential revenue return.

The political elite's reluctance to address the water
crisis is also influenced by their vested interests. Many
politicians and influential figures have direct or indirect
stakes in the agricultural sector, benefiting from the current
system of subsidies and water pricing. This conflict of
interest prevents meaningful reforms and perpetuates the
cycle of water mismanagement and scarcity.

Pakistan's dependence on water-intensive crops
exacerbates its water crisis, creating a troubling paradox
where the nation's scarce water resources are allocated to
crops that yield minimal economic return. The
inefficiencies and economic disincentives embedded in this
system reflect broader issues within Pakistan's agricultural
policies and highlight a critical disconnect between
resource use and economic benefit.

Producing one kilogram of tomatoes requires
approximately 180 liters of water, while the water footprint

for cotton is alarmingly high: around 9,800 liters per kilogram. Given that a kilogram of cotton sells for about $0.71 in the international market,[10] Pakistan is effectively expending vast quantities of fresh water for an inconsequential revenue return. This situation epitomizes what one prominent U.S. politician described as *"the worst trade deal in the history of trade deals, maybe ever."* The vast discrepancy between water use and economic gain underscores a system that is not only unsustainable but also economically irrational.

At this juncture, it might appear more sensible to consider selling fresh water to neighboring markets, such as the Gulf States, where water scarcity is acute and demand is high. The economic incentives for such a trade could potentially offset the losses incurred from producing low-value, water-intensive crops.

However, entrenched interests within Pakistan's political and economic spheres persist in promoting and expanding the cultivation of these crops.

Pakistan's focus on cotton has made it the largest exporter of virtual groundwater worldwide, surpassing both the United States and India. Despite this, plans are underway to double cotton production by 2025.

---

[10] Sattar, U. (2023). Pakistan's political economy perpetuates its water crisis. Stimson.

The dominance of sugar mills and cotton plantations, which partially finance many of Pakistan's mainstream political parties, is a significant factor in this continued focus.

A closer look at the political economy reveals that approximately 40 of Pakistan's 89 sugar mills are owned by the political elite and their families. These corporate farming practices have not only entrenched the cultivation of sugar but also elevated Pakistan to the status of the fifth-largest sugar producer globally. Similarly, Pakistan's focus on cotton has made it the largest exporter of virtual groundwater worldwide, surpassing both the United States and India. The country exports about 13 million acre-feet (MAF) of its water supply through cotton-based textiles annually. Despite this, plans are underway to double cotton production by 2025 to boost exports and foreign exchange reserves. In practical terms, Pakistan exports between two to three times the amount of water needed to meet domestic demand each year.

In 2017, Pakistan ranked eighth lowest globally in terms of water productivity, generating only $1.4 per cubic meter of water withdrawn compared to the world average of $13.6 per cubic meter.

The entrenchment of sugar and cotton cultivation in Pakistan is the result of decades of favorable government policies, including subsidies and price fixing. These policies have artificially propped up the profitability of these crops while discouraging more water-efficient alternatives. The irrigation system, one of the most inefficient globally, operates at just 39 percent efficiency. This is a direct consequence of aging infrastructure and inadequate maintenance, with 61 percent of water lost during conveyance through canals, distributaries, minors, and watercourses, and during field application.

Pakistan's agricultural sector, despite its substantial contribution to the employment of some 120 million people, suffers from low water productivity. In 2017, Pakistan ranked eighth lowest globally in terms of water productivity, generating only $1.4 per cubic meter of water withdrawn compared to the world average of $13.6 per cubic meter. The country's performance in wastewater treatment is also concerning, **with only 1 percent of collected wastewater treated, placing Pakistan among the lowest in terms of water treatment rates.** For comparison, over 63 percent of globally produced wastewater is collected, 52 percent is treated, and 11 percent is reused.

The economic inefficiency extends to the broader fiscal implications. Despite the farm sector accounting for one-fifth of GDP and nearly half of national employment, it contributes less than 0.1 percent to total tax revenues. This meager contribution fails to provide adequate financing for the maintenance of the irrigation infrastructure, exacerbating the inefficiencies and losses within the system.

The cotton industry, while contributing significantly to exports, constitutes a minuscule portion of Pakistan's GDP – only 0.6 percent.[11] This disparity highlights the low value of Pakistan's exports both domestically and internationally. The focus on water-intensive crops,

---

[11] Country Report of Pakistan. (2023). Country statement of Pakistan for 81st plenary meeting of ICAC

therefore, has led to Pakistan having the world's highest water intensity rate – the amount of water used per unit of GDP. It reflects an economy that is extraordinarily water-hungry.

Given the low value of cotton and other water-intensive crops, the current export policies do not offer a viable solution for Pakistan's long-term economic or water security. The focus should shift towards sectors that provide higher value and require less water. For instance, the service and IT sectors have shown substantial growth and potential. Knowledge-intensive exports, which grew from 10 percent of all service exports in 2010 to 50 percent in 2020, now rival the value of all of Pakistan's vegetable sectors combined. Encouraging policies that support high-value goods, services, and information technology should be prioritized over those geared toward exporting low-value, water-intensive products like knitwear, bedwear, and towels.

The consequences of political apathy towards the water crisis are severe and far-reaching. Without immediate and sustained action, Pakistan faces the threat of severe water shortages, economic instability, and social unrest. The rural population, heavily reliant on agriculture for their livelihoods, will bear the brunt, facing increased poverty and migration to urban areas. This migration will further strain already overburdened cities, intensifying issues such as unemployment, inadequate housing, and poor sanitation.

The entrenched interests in the sugar and cotton industries, coupled with the inefficiencies in water management and agricultural productivity, have created a system that is both economically unsustainable and environmentally damaging. The political elite's reluctance to address these issues reflects a broader failure to prioritize long-term national interests over short-term gains. To ensure a sustainable future, Pakistan must undertake a comprehensive overhaul of its agricultural policies, redirecting focus towards water-efficient practices and high-value sectors that align with both economic and environmental sustainability.

Pakistan's reliance on water-intensive crops and outdated irrigation practices is a fundamental issue that contributes to its water crisis. The political and economic systems in place reinforce these practices, despite their evident drawbacks. Shifting focus towards more sustainable agricultural practices and high-value sectors could offer a path to economic stability and water security. Without such a shift, Pakistan's water crisis will continue to escalate, with dire consequences for its economy and its people.

Chaper 6: Water Wars

In February 2024, India's decision to halt the flow of the Ravi River into Pakistan marked a significant escalation in the ongoing water disputes between the two countries. Citing its exclusive rights under the Indus Water Treaty (IWT), India's action has been characterized as "water terrorism" by Pakistani media, reflecting the heightened tensions surrounding this critical resource. This incident underscores a broader, chronic issue: the fierce competition over shared water resources in a region where both countries face growing water scarcity.

The Indus Water Treaty, signed in 1960, was a landmark agreement brokered by the World Bank to address the distribution of the Indus River system's waters between India and Pakistan. The treaty allocated the waters of the eastern rivers – the Ravi, Beas, and Sutlej – to India, while Pakistan was given control over the western rivers – the Indus, Jhelum, and Chenab. Despite being hailed as a diplomatic triumph, the treaty has not prevented periodic tensions over water rights.

The roots of the water dispute between India and Pakistan can be traced back to the partition of British India in 1947. The division of the Indus River system, which flows through both nations, was a contentious issue during the partition. The river system is a lifeline for Pakistan, providing 80% of its surface water. This dependency has made water a strategic asset, and any disruption in its flow has far-reaching implications for Pakistan's agriculture, industry, and overall stability.

The 1960 Indus Water Treaty was designed to prevent conflict over water resources by clearly delineating water-sharing rights. However, it has not been without its challenges. Disputes have periodically arisen over issues such as dam construction, river diversion, and treaty compliance. For instance, India's construction of the Baglihar Dam and the Kishanganga Dam on the Chenab and Jhelum rivers, respectively, raised concerns in Pakistan about potential reductions in river flow and the impact on its agricultural and economic needs.

In recent years, as both nations face increasing water stress due to climate change, population growth, and mismanagement, these historical tensions have been exacerbated. The 2024 decision by India to stop the flow of the Ravi River represents a dramatic shift from previous patterns of water diplomacy, indicating a new phase of heightened competition and conflict over shared water resources.

The cessation of the Ravi River's flow into Pakistan is a particularly alarming development given the current state of water scarcity in both countries. Water scarcity in South Asia is a growing crisis, driven by factors such as over-extraction of water resources, inefficient irrigation practices, pollution, and the effects of climate change. The Indus River system, already strained, is critical to the livelihoods of millions of people in both India and Pakistan.

For Pakistan, the Ravi River is a crucial source of water for the Punjab region, which is the country's primary agricultural zone. The river supports irrigation for crops, drinking water for communities, and industrial uses. A disruption in its flow impacts food security, economic stability, and overall national security. The cessation of the river's flow could lead to reduced agricultural output, higher food prices, and increased rural poverty, exacerbating existing economic challenges.

India's move to halt the Ravi River's flow could also trigger a cascade of geopolitical and environmental consequences. Pakistan's response to this act of "water terrorism" may involve escalating diplomatic and possibly military tensions. Historically, water disputes have been a flashpoint for broader conflicts between the two countries, and the latest development could further strain already fragile relations.

Such actions by both governments reflect a short-sighted and counterproductive approach, ignoring the greater need for cooperation in managing shared resources for mutual benefit.

Neeraj Singh Manhas, a Special Advisor for South Asia at the Parley Policy Initiative, Republic of Korea and expert on Hydrodiplomacy and Water Security in South Asia, makes note of the common enemy crisis facing both countries and their increasingly desperate populations. *"There are significant similarities between Pakistan and India regarding the water crisis. Both countries are facing severe water scarcity issues, largely due to increasing populations, climate change, and inefficient water management. They share transboundary river systems like the Indus, making their water issues interconnected. The depletion of groundwater, agricultural overuse, and erratic monsoon seasons are common challenges in both countries, leading to a growing concern over sustainable water management."*

India, despite its significant water resources, faces severe regional imbalances and pollution issues. The country's burgeoning population and rapid economic growth have strained its water infrastructure, leading to shortages in several states. The water scarcity issues in India, combined with its strategic moves over the Indus system, create a complex dynamic where both nations are increasingly vying for control over limited resources. As Neeraj pointed out, *"When it comes to Pakistan, the historical tensions over the Indus Waters Treaty complicate matters. While India's internal water policies may not be at odds with Pakistan, the shared rivers and the political context of water rights often create friction between the two nations."*

The impact of worsening water crises on regional stability cannot be overstated. As both India and Pakistan face mounting water stress, their strategies for managing and controlling water resources may become more aggressive. This competition could lead to more frequent and severe disputes, with potential repercussions for regional security and economic development. Water scarcity could also amplify existing social and political tensions within both countries, further destabilizing the region.

The international community's role in mediating these disputes is crucial but challenging. While the Indus Water Treaty was a significant achievement in conflict resolution, its effectiveness in the current context is uncertain. The treaty's mechanisms for dispute resolution and arbitration may be tested as both nations navigate the complexities of modern water management and escalating tensions.

The historic tensions over water, exacerbated by current environmental and geopolitical challenges, pose a serious threat to regional stability. As the water crisis deepens, the potential for conflict over shared resources increases, making it imperative for both nations –and the international community – to seek sustainable solutions to prevent further escalation and ensure equitable access to water resources.

Nevertheless, some like Neeraj Singh Manhas remain positive for future cooperation and thus potentially a de-escalation. He talks to us saying, *"There is potential for cooperation [between the neighboring countries], particularly in agriculture, where both countries face similar challenges. Sharing water management technologies could be mutually beneficial, especially in improving irrigation efficiency and managing water resources more sustainably. While political tensions may make collaboration difficult, water technology and agricultural practices could provide a neutral platform for cooperation between the two countries, offering solutions to a common crisis."* Tech diplomacy may pave the way for political de-escalation as well.

Another possible flashpoint could arise on Pakistan's Western border. Pakistan and Afghanistan share the waters of the Kabul River, a vital lifeline flowing through both countries.

The Kabul River, originating in the Hindu Kush mountains in Afghanistan, flows into Pakistan, where it merges with the Swat River and its tributaries before joining the Indus River at Attock. **This river basin supports the livelihoods of approximately 25 million people in Pakistan, a number projected to increase to 37**

million by 2050. The river's waters are crucial for agriculture, drinking water, and industrial use.

The lack of a formal agreement on water sharing adds complexity to an already tense relationship. Historically, water disputes have been significant sources of conflict worldwide, and the Kabul River could become another flashpoint for rising geopolitical tensions and border instability between the two nations.

Afghanistan, seeking to develop its water resources, has undertaken several dam construction projects on the Kabul River. These projects, while vital for Afghanistan's development and energy needs, could significantly impact the downstream flow into Pakistan. The potential reduction in water flow can lead to diminished agricultural yields, power shortages, and increased competition for the already scarce water resources in Pakistan.

While the lack of a water-sharing agreement poses significant risks, it also provides a chance for Pakistan and Afghanistan to engage in constructive dialogue and cooperation. However, as the hour grows more desperate, the risk is there of a unilateral course of action by these two countries, even if it comes to the determinant of the other.

But the risk for conflict will not be limited between states, but also go within states. The former can be avoided if cool minds prevail, while the latter remains a far more complex and unpredictable challenge.

In a country grappling with homegrown Islamic militancy and a disturbing rise in extremism, Pakistan faces a multifaceted crisis where water scarcity intertwines with the dynamics of terrorism. While water shortage may not be the direct root cause of terrorism, it acts as a powerful destabilizing force, creating conditions that enable violent extremist organizations to thrive. This complex interplay between water scarcity and terrorism unfolds in two significant ways: by exacerbating the conditions conducive to radicalization and by providing opportunities for terrorists to exploit resource scarcity for their own gain.

In the face of such economic hardship, extremist groups find fertile ground for recruitment. These organizations often present themselves as alternative sources of support or ideological refuge, particularly to those who feel abandoned by their government.

Water scarcity, as a crisis multiplier, intensifies existing social and economic tensions. When communities face severe shortages of this essential resource, their ability to sustain livelihoods diminishes, pushing them towards increasingly desperate measures. This exacerbates existing vulnerabilities and may drive individuals to seek alternatives outside the bounds of legality or stability. In many rural areas of Pakistan, where agriculture is the primary source of employment, water shortages have a profound impact. Agriculture is not only a major provider of jobs but also a cornerstone of rural economies. Droughts and inadequate water supply disrupt agricultural activities, leading to job losses and heightened poverty.

In the face of such economic hardship, extremist groups find fertile ground for recruitment. These organizations often present themselves as alternative sources of support or ideological refuge, particularly to those who feel abandoned by their government.

For instance, during severe droughts and flooding, communities that have lost their agricultural livelihoods may find the promises of extremist groups appealing, as these groups offer immediate financial relief or ideological solace. This dynamic was evident following the devastating floods in Pakistan in 2010 when Jamaat-ud-Dawa, the front organization of the terrorist group Lashkar-e-Taiba, provided significant humanitarian aid. This act, while appearing as a charitable gesture, was a strategic move to gain influence and recruit individuals from among the most vulnerable populations.

The nexus between water scarcity and terrorism is further complicated by demographic pressures and climate change. Pakistan's rapid population growth exacerbates the strain on scarce resources, leading to heightened competition for water and land. This increased pressure can foster tensions between communities, creating an environment ripe for conflict and extremist recruitment. Young people facing bleak prospects and limited economic opportunities may be more susceptible to radicalization, as extremist groups offer not only financial incentives but also a sense of purpose or belonging.

The regional context adds another layer of complexity. The ongoing conflict over water resources between Pakistan and its neighboring countries, particularly India, intensifies the scarcity issues. India's construction of dams on the Indus River's tributaries has significantly reduced the flow of water into Pakistan. This competition for water resources, combined with the broader impacts of climate change, exacerbates existing conflicts and contributes to regional instability. The reduced water availability threatens agricultural productivity and heightens socio-economic tensions within Pakistan, creating additional opportunities for extremist groups to exploit.

The impact of water scarcity on terrorism is evident in how it intersects with broader socio-economic factors. The disruptions caused by water shortages not only undermine agricultural productivity but also contribute to increased poverty and unemployment. In regions where legal economic opportunities are scarce, the appeal of extremist groups can become stronger. These groups may exploit the grievances of marginalized communities, using promises of financial support or ideological motives to recruit disillusioned individuals.

Furthermore, the demographic explosion in Pakistan adds to the challenges. As the population continues to grow, the pressure on already limited resources intensifies. This demographic shift exacerbates competition for water and land, fueling tensions that can contribute to conflict and instability. Extremist groups often target these vulnerabilities, using resource scarcity and socio-economic hardship as tools for recruitment and radicalization.

The role of extremist organizations in exploiting water scarcity is also evident in their ability to step into gaps left by governments. In areas where state support is insufficient or absent, extremist groups may provide humanitarian aid or services, gaining influence and loyalty from affected communities. This was the case with Jamaat-ud-Dawa, which capitalized on the aftermath of natural disasters to strengthen its foothold and recruit new members.

The interplay between water scarcity and terrorism underscores the need for comprehensive strategies that address both immediate and long-term impacts. Governments must improve their ability to provide humanitarian relief and support vulnerable communities to reduce the appeal of extremist groups. Effective water management practices, investment in sustainable agriculture, and regional cooperation on transboundary water issues are essential components of a holistic approach to mitigating the impact of water scarcity.

International collaboration is also crucial in managing shared water resources and addressing the broader effects of climate change. By working together to improve water management and address the root causes of instability, nations can create a more stable and secure environment. This, in turn, can help reduce the conditions that foster radicalization and extremist activities.

The consequences of ignoring the relationship between water scarcity and terrorism are severe. Without addressing the underlying issues of resource management and socio-economic disparity, Pakistan and other affected regions face a future of escalating conflict and instability. The interplay between water scarcity and extremism highlights the urgent need for integrated solutions that tackle both the immediate impacts of resource shortages and the broader socio-economic factors that contribute to radicalization.

Moreover, the cyclical nature of these crises underscores a disheartening reality: **while the dire need for comprehensive reforms is evident, the political will to implement them often falters.** As we transition to the next chapter, we delve into the political arena where grand promises are made in the face of growing desperation, yet tangible change remains elusive. This exploration reveals the disconnect between political rhetoric and the harsh realities faced by the people, painting a sobering picture of unfulfilled commitments and ongoing struggles.

Chapter 7: New Promises, Old Story

Desperation makes the best customers. A worsening crisis only makes people desperate for rapid solutions – solutions that can be promised and profited off. Politicians, with their promises of grand projects and sweeping reforms, have found fertile ground in Pakistan's water crisis to further their own interests. Each election cycle brings with it new pledges to solve the water shortage, yet the situation remains the same and dire. The promises are enticing, and the people, in their desperation, often cling to these assurances, only to be let down time and time again.

Through loans and taxpayer money, millions of dollars are being poured into water utility projects under the guise of making them 'better'. The reality, however, is that the situation only worsens. Residents are all too familiar with the cycle of big promises followed by disappointing outcomes.

"The infrastructure was built years ago, but it was only operational for two days, never again," said Asadullah Khan, a resident of Baldia Town, as he dragged a drum of water toward his house. This sentiment is echoed across Karachi, where grand infrastructure projects like the Greater Karachi Water Supply Scheme, or K-IV, have become emblematic of political exploitation.

The K-IV scheme, launched almost two decades ago, was heralded as the solution to Karachi's perennial water woes. Funded by the Federal government and managed by the Water and Power Development Authority (WAPDA), the project was designed to supply the remaining 650 million gallons per day (MGD) of water needed by the city's residents. However, today, the scheme remains a distant dream, with only 10 percent of the work completed. Despite foreign aid and taxpayer money being allocated, little has materialized. Instead, the project has become a symbol of corruption and inefficiency.

Each new promise of an infrastructure project comes with a corresponding increase in funds allocated, and each time, the outcome is the same: incomplete projects and misappropriated funds. The populace, desperate for relief, continues to hope that this time, things will be different.

The goal is never to provide a lasting solution because a lasting solution is not profitable. Instead, politicians make big infrastructure promises that are always meant to be broken. The K-IV scheme, for instance, has been inaugurated multiple times over the years. Each time, funds are released, only to be quickly siphoned into deep pockets. In February this year, during the 10th Provincial Coordination and Implementation Committee (PCIC) meeting, it was reported that only 10 percent of the work on phase one of the project had been completed, using the released amount of Rs23.1 billion. This pattern of incomplete projects and misallocated funds is all too familiar to Karachi's residents.

Despite the dismal progress, calls for more funding persist. The Government of Sindh is now asking the federal government to release an additional Rs45 billion to continue the work. These requests for funds often come without accountability for the previous amounts already spent. The cycle of requesting, receiving, and misusing funds continues unabated, enriching those in power while leaving the residents in a perpetual state of need.

This manipulation extends beyond just one project. Across Pakistan, similar stories unfold as politicians leverage the water crisis for personal gain. Each new promise of an infrastructure project comes with a corresponding increase in funds allocated, and each time, the outcome is the same: incomplete projects and misappropriated funds. The populace, desperate for relief, continues to hope that this time, things will be different.

In Lahore, the 'Saaf Pani' (clean water) Project stands as another glaring example of how politicians exploit water crises for personal and political gains. Launched two decades ago during Pervez Musharraf's presidency, the project involved establishing water filtration plants in 26 districts at the cost of billions of rupees. These plants were celebrated as a one-time investment for everlasting good, but the reality was far from the promise. Without a budget or plan for filter replacement and management, the filters soon became choked, and water supply was disrupted. There were no arrangements for supervision, maintenance, or security, and when Musharraf left office, the plants were vandalized and left in disrepair.

Then came the turn of the elected governments. Rather than fixing the existing filtration plants, the new administration decided to build new ones nearby, initiating 'Saaf Pani' Round II. **Billions were spent again, only for these new plants to meet the same fate: choked filters, disrepear, and vandalism.**

More recently, 'Saaf Pani' Round III has been launched, with yet more promises of providing clean drinking water to the public, perpetuating the cycle of grand promises and disappointing results.

The Lower Bari Doab Canal (LBOD) project is another historical example of mismanaged water projects. Commenced on December 13, 1984, with a World Bank/IDA credit of $150 million, the LBOD project was initially estimated to cost over Rs8.5 billion but ended up costing over Rs31 billion. The project left behind a trail of engineering, environmental, human, and socio-economic failures.

Stage 1 of the LBOD project aimed to raise agricultural production in about 1.27 million Cultivable Command Area, mainly by reducing waterlogging and salinity in Nawabshah, Sanghar, and Mirpurkhas districts. Major donors included the International Development Association (IDA) and the Asian Development Bank (ADB). However, the project's unfinished work was merged into another mega project, the National Drainage Project (NDP), costing $786 million. This project extended the LBOD to cater to the effluent generated in Punjab through a 1,464 km long drain under the National Surface Drainage System (NSDS).

Badin district was used as a conduit for the Spinal Drain of the project, meant to dispose of saline effluent to the Arabian Sea through a 42 km long Tidal Link Canal. Despite local protests, the top management decided to transport the effluent via the Tidal Link canal, crossing a natural lake complex of significant ecological importance. This complex supported the livelihoods of about 15,000 fishermen from 40 villages.

The decision to transport effluent through this delicate ecosystem required diligent environmental and socio-economic mechanisms, which were glaringly absent. The World Bank Inspection Panel's draft report noted that the selected alignment for the Tidal Link was "politically attractive" but technically and environmentally risky.

Ignoring warnings, the project used non-cohesive soil for the channel bed and embankments, leaving the structures vulnerable to tidal wave action. The Tidal Link was also aligned against the wind direction, adding pressure to tidal inflow from the sea creek. On June 24, 1998, the Cholri Weir collapsed, unleashing unprecedented environmental havoc. The fragile lake system was converted into a saline sink beyond recovery. Authorities made cosmetic efforts to repair the weir, but within four months, the breach widened to 450 ft, and the situation became beyond saving.

Yet, that was not the climax of the story, a disastrous cyclone lashed the area on May 21, 1999. It caused 54 breaches in the embankment of the tidal link rendering it completely irreparable. The breached structure unleashed an unprecedented disaster on nearby settlements of fishermen communities and according to official figures, about 75 people died in Badin alone, whereas local communities put the toll on a much higher side. With this disaster, embankments were washed away the Tidal Link flow became part of the dhand complex, and salinity levels started rising, thus playing havoc with the environment.

At one stage, the salinity of Pateji Dhand was measured at a horrifying 68,000 ppm, compared to its previous measurement of 15,000 ppm. To put this into perspective, the salinity of the sea is around 35,000 ppm, meaning Pateji Dhand had become doubly saline. The World Bank Inspection Panel document aptly describes the dhand as "biologically dead". Before the LBOD project, the lake system received low salinity water from local drains in Badin, part of the Kotri Surface Drainage System. However, these drains began to reverse flow, particularly during high tide, spilling into surrounding agricultural land and rendering it unfit for cropping.

The poor communities of Badin not only lost their fisheries and other resources from the dhands but also began losing their agricultural land due to backflow in local drains connected to the dhand complex. This backflow also impacted the aquifer in the vicinity, depriving communities of drinkable fresh water.

The latest in the line of 'new promises' is the Diamer-Bhasha Dam. **This ambitious project, if completed, would be the biggest dam in Pakistan and the tallest RCC (Roller Compacted Concrete) dam in the world.** It aims to extend the life of Tarbela Dam located downstream by 35 years, control flood damage by the River Indus during high floods, produce 4800 megawatts of electricity through hydropower generation, and deliver storage of an extra 10.5 cubic kilometers (8,500,000 acre-feet) of water for irrigation and drinking purposes.

However, a scandal over the funds collected for the construction of the dam has emerged, pointing fingers at the former dispensation of Imran Khan and former Chief Justice Saqib Nisar. The then CJP had initiated a fund-raising campaign for the Diamer-Bhasha and Mohmand dams in July 2018, later joined by the then Prime Minister Imran Khan, to overcome the country's water scarcity. It was claimed that $40 million had been collected as donations for the dam, but $63 million was spent on advertisements promoting it. Additionally, salaries of state employees were deducted and contributed as donations for the dam. However, since Chief Justice Saqib Nisar's retirement, enthusiasm for the fund dwindled, and donations nearly stopped.

The Diamer-Bhasha Dam project had actually been proposed since the 1980s. In 1998, Prime Minister Nawaz Sharif inaugurated the project, but it was only green-lit by President Pervez Musharraf's government in 2006. It remained stalled due to the World Bank and IMF's refusal to provide funds for the project. Actual construction began only in May 2020, when China stepped in to help Pakistan with the construction. The Pakistani government then signed a Rs 442 billion contract with a joint venture of China Power and Frontier Works Organisation (FWO) for the dam's construction.

Successive governments have touted the dam as a solution to the country's water problems. However, what is overlooked in political rhetoric is the dam's potential to be an ecological disaster. Reportedly, a letter written by the original designer of the dam in 2004 to then Pakistan President Pervez Musharraf read, *"I shudder at the thought of earthquake effects on Bhasha. Dam-burst would wipe out Tarbela and all barrages on Indus; which would take us back to the stone-age."*

Further, in a September 2018 letter addressed to the then Chief Justice of Pakistan, one of the US' foremost design and infrastructure firms, AECOM, cautioned against the Diamer-Bhasha Dam. The letter stated, *"If Water and Power Development Authority (WAPDA) decides to proceed with this concept, the cost would be exorbitant and construction time would exceed ten years. The project risk associated with an RCC dam is extremely high due to the transportation issue and seismic profile found at the location of the project. In summation, for practical and economic reasons, the RCC dam should not be recommended for the DBD project."*

Nevertheless, the heavily indebted Pakistani government has been aggressively seeking further loans to fund this project. The total cost of the project is estimated at $12.6 billion, but the country's poor state of the economy and worsening image of corruption have reduced its credit score to junk status. Pakistan's junk credit rating becomes a hurdle in acquiring $3.5 billion in debt for the Diamer-Bhasha Dam project. International credit rating agencies have assigned a junk rating to Pakistan, describing the country's debt as highly risky. This has now become the biggest stumbling block in acquiring new foreign commercial loans and floating sovereign bonds.

Pakistan requested $3.5 billion in financing from its long-time ally, the Kingdom of Saudi Arabia (KSA), for the Diamer-Bhasha Dam when a delegation visited them from the country. Out of $3.5 billion, WAPDA asked the KSA authorities to provide a concessional loan of $2.3 billion at a 2.25% interest rate for 25 years with a grace period of six years. It sought $1.2 billion as its equity in the project at 4.45%, on par with the interest cost of a US 10-year Treasury Bond.

A project of this magnitude in such a fragile zone could either propel the nation forward or cripple its future. Ultimately, the outcome hinges on how the government chooses to allocate the funds it receives. Will it invest in building a strong infrastructure that will serve Pakistan for generations, or will the project become bogged down by corruption scandals and political infighting, leading to decades of additional delays – delays the country cannot afford?

Some, like Naseer Memon, hold a pessimistic view of the situation. Having served in various capacities within multiple development initiatives, he reflects on stalled progress, stating, *"Every province agreed to it. It was approved through all platforms, but 20 years have passed, and it's still under process. At its current pace, I don't think it will be completed in the next 20 years either."*

His remarks highlight the deep-rooted bureaucratic inefficiencies and lack of urgency that have hindered crucial water management projects, further exacerbating Pakistan's crisis.

Memon also raises doubts about the seriousness of efforts to manage Pakistan's water crisis. *"You asked if anyone at a higher level is genuinely committed to addressing water issues. The answer is no. Unfortunately, there is a lack of serious and meaningful effort. The federal government needs to take an objective and impartial stance on these controversial matters, with the goal of defusing tensions. But a large portion of resources is funneled into defense and other systems, which means water issues are not prioritized. It seems the government is distracted by several other pressing matters."*

The exploitation of water crises by politicians for personal and political gain has long been a trend in Pakistan. Projects like the K-IV scheme, the Diamer-Bhasha Dam, and the 'Saaf Pani' initiative have repeatedly fallen short of their promises, leaving communities to bear the brunt of their failures. While these projects are often touted as solutions to the country's water problems, they often result in environmental and economic disasters due to poor planning, corruption, and mismanagement.

The need for a shift in approach is urgent. Sustainable and well-planned solutions must be prioritized over short-term political gains. This includes investing in robust infrastructure, ensuring transparency and accountability in the use of funds, and involving local communities in decision-making processes.

As Memon notes, *"The water equivalent to almost five Kalabagh Dams is being wasted into the Arabian Sea, and yet we continue to fight over the remaining potential of the Kalabagh Dam itself. In conclusion, while there's much debate, there is little in terms of serious, coordinated effort to address the issue."*

Yet, as we look at the current picture, one cannot help but ponder a critical question: Can Pakistan even break free from its history of unfulfilled promises and leverage this moment to foster real change, or will it remain trapped in a cycle of political exploitation and public desperation? The future of Pakistan's water crisis – and the well-being of its people – hinges on the answer to this pressing question.

Chapter 8: Water on Roads, Not in Taps

If you are to truly comprehend the gross mismanagement of Karachi's water resources, all you need to do is wait for the monsoons. The city's water crisis is not just a matter of scarcity but also one of severe misallocation and incompetence. In upscale neighborhoods like Clifton and Defence Housing Authority (DHA), where house prices regularly fetch a million dollars – a fortune for most in this country – the situation is paradoxical. **Taps remain dry while the roads get flooded during monsoon rains.**

For these wealthy residents, it is a case of *"water, water everywhere and not a drop to drink."* Approximately 45,000 household units in Defence Housing Authority (DHA) and Cantonment Board Clifton (CBC) have been facing an acute water crisis. While it is common knowledge that residents of Karachi's posh Defence Housing Authority are always complaining about water shortages, it was hoped that the rise in the water table following the heavy monsoon rains in 2022 would see an improvement in supply. However, nothing of the sort has happened so far, as highlighted in a recent news piece.

Sikandar Kazi, a longtime resident of DHA, recalls a time when the water supply was sufficient. *"Many years ago, we used to get sufficient water, three times a week. But things started changing some 15 years ago when we started getting water twice a week and then once a week. Now it is once or twice a month, bringing on an acute water shortage,"* he laments.

The deteriorating situation has forced residents like Sikandar to rely heavily on water tankers, an expensive and unsustainable solution.

Mehdi Abbas, a resident of 23rd Street in Phase 5, echoes similar frustrations. *"We get water through the lines only twice a month. And that, too, only for one hour, which amounts to nothing. It doesn't fulfill our household needs unless we arrange for a tanker,"* he says. Adding to the woes, the quality of water that does reach these homes is often questionable. *"Sometimes the water that we get through the pipeline is mixed with sewage, but no action is taken regarding this issue even after complaining to the CBC. I have had to get my water tanks cleaned due to this,"* Mehdi adds.

The Defence Housing Authority was initially conceived as a well-planned housing society, keeping in consideration the number of residents per house and their water needs. However, those plans seem to have long been discarded.

"It is not possible for a family of five to live on 2,000 gallons a month," remarks Sikandar. The water supply infrastructure, once robust, now suffers from various issues such as the need for maintenance work on filtration plants or pumping stations. Breakages in supply lines are also a frequent occurrence. When these lines are broken, the water supply is simply stopped, exacerbating the shortage.

Rumors allege that the authorities deliberately break the supply lines to facilitate the tanker mafia, who allegedly share a cut of their profits with the provincial government. This theory, while unproven, resonates with many residents who see no other explanation for the persistent water shortages and the thriving business of water tankers. *"And since DHA residents can afford tankers during any kind of water shortage, we are also in a way facilitating the tanker mafia. Our buying power is hurting us while if the same thing happens in Clifton or PECHS, they will conserve water and not immediately go for buying water from tankers,"* Sikandar explains.

The situation in Karachi's upscale neighborhoods highlights a broader issue of water mismanagement and corruption that affects the entire city. The disparity between the availability of water during monsoon floods and the scarcity during dry months underscores the need for a more effective water management system. As residents of affluent areas struggle to secure clean water, the city's poor suffer even more, often unable to afford the costly water tankers.

Meanwhile, on the roads, luxury cars drive over sewage water. The gutter (sewage) lines have been choked, causing sewage water to overflow onto the streets. When it rains, the gutters overflow, leading to widespread street flooding. In other places, a little rain qualifies as pleasant or gloomy weather, depending on preferences. **In Karachi, the city's residents have to prepare for a war.**

Streets transform into rivers, making transportation nearly impossible. Public transport grinds to a halt, and those who venture out face significant risks. Cars often stall in knee-deep water, and motorcycles struggle to navigate the inundated roads.

All local bodies, hospitals, the water board, energy suppliers, and cantonments are instructed ahead of the predicted event. Authorities also advise citizens to stay indoors and take care of their children during this period. Rescue 1122 is put on high alert. Employees may take leave or work from home, provided they have a backup power supply. As it rains, the streets become flooded within hours. A blackout may also ensue as the water level rises. This is a yearly occurrence in a city of some 35 million souls.

The lack of proper drainage and sewage systems exacerbates the situation. Streets transform into rivers, making transportation nearly impossible. Public transport grinds to a halt, and those who venture out face significant risks. Cars often stall in knee-deep water, and motorcycles struggle to navigate the inundated roads. This not only disrupts daily life but also poses serious health risks. Stagnant water becomes a breeding ground for mosquitoes, leading to outbreaks of diseases such as dengue and malaria.

Efforts to address the situation have been a piecemeal at best. The government's response has often been reactive rather than proactive. Plans to upgrade the drainage system or improve water supply infrastructure are announced with much fanfare but see little implementation. Corruption and bureaucratic inefficiencies further hinder progress. As a result, each monsoon season brings the same cycle of flooding, water shortages, and public outrage.

This situation of water on roads, and not in taps seems to have even reached the heart of the nation's capital. Islamabad, a city long considered a symbol of order and affluence in Pakistan, is no longer immune to the debilitating water shortages that plague the rest of the country. While the elite sectors, home to influential diplomats and high-ranking officials, may still enjoy some measure of water security, the majority of the city is grappling with a severe shortage that has become a daily struggle for its residents.

In some cases, people have been forced to queue outside the CDA offices at the crack of dawn, starting as early as 4 AM, in hopes of securing a portion of the meager water supply available.

The crisis is particularly acute in the 'G' and 'I' sectors of Islamabad, which have been hit hard by water scarcity. These areas, once considered prime real estate, are now characterized by long periods of dry taps and unreliable water supply. Even parts of the F sectors, which run parallel to the bustling Margalla Road, are experiencing shortages. In F-8, there are streets where residents have not received any water from the Capital Development Authority (CDA) for years. This dire situation has forced many households to invest heavily in groundwater extraction, leading to soaring electricity costs and the gradual depletion of the city's water table.

For many residents, the solution to this crisis involves purchasing water from private tanker contractors, an expensive alternative that can cost upwards of Rs. 3000 for a single tanker load. This not only places a financial burden on residents but also contributes to a growing sense of frustration and helplessness. In some cases, people have been forced to queue outside the CDA offices at the crack of dawn, starting as early as 4 AM, in hopes of securing a portion of the meager water supply available. For a deposit of Rs. 100, they might receive around 20% of a tanker's capacity – a quantity that is barely sufficient for basic needs such as cooking and washing.

The demand for water in Islamabad is further compounded by the city's rapidly growing population. With an annual growth rate of over five percent, Islamabad's population has surged to approximately 1.75 million. This demographic boom places additional strain on the city's already overstretched water infrastructure, exacerbating the shortages and highlighting the urgent need for effective management and investment in water resources.

The irony of the situation is that while taps run dry in the capital, other parts of the country are regularly inundated with floodwater. The most devastating example of this was the 2022 flood, which was catastrophic in scale. Satellite imagery revealed that a third of Pakistan was submerged, with a new 100km wide inland lake forming in Sindh Province. **This disaster impacted 33 million people, with more than 1,700 lives lost and 3,554 individuals injured. The** scale of the destruction pushed an estimated 8-9 million people into poverty, further exacerbating the country's socio-economic challenges.

However, Pakistan's vulnerability to floods is not a recent phenomenon. The country has a long history of deadly floods, with significant events recorded as far back as 2010, when flooding in Khyber Pakhtunkhwa, Punjab, and Balochistan claimed 1,985 lives between July and August. Flooding has continued to be a recurring issue each year from 2001 to 2021. The frequency and severity of these events have only intensified due to climate change, which brings more rainfall and accelerates glacial melting. Yet, Pakistan's approach to managing these disasters has remained largely unchanged, marked by inaction and ineffective policies.

Climate change undeniably exacerbates the frequency and severity of natural disasters like flooding, but it would be an oversimplification to attribute the human cost of the 2022 floods solely to global warming. The significant damage caused by the floods is also a result of inadequate domestic policies and a lack of preparedness. The National Flood Protection Program, designed to span from 2015 to 2025, acknowledges the impacts of climate change, deforestation, and the use of flood plains. It presents a range of solutions aimed at mitigating these issues. Yet, despite being drafted in 2015, approved in 2017, and submitted for financing in 2019, the program is yet to be implemented.

The World Bank's contribution of $250 million for a sustainable water management program was suspended in 2019 due to project management issues. The suspension highlights the persistent problems in implementing effective water management strategies. Additionally, little has been done to address deforestation along Pakistan's watersheds, which is a critical issue. Clear-cutting leads to poor water quality, increased erosion, and the destruction of natural ecosystems that play a vital role in absorbing the impacts of floods. Without significant efforts to address these problems, Pakistan remains ill-equipped to manage and mitigate the effects of flooding.

The 2022 flooding situation was exacerbated by a lack of preventative measures and an ineffective response to previous disasters. The monsoon rains that inundated Pakistan were not unprecedented; the country has experienced similar rainfall events in the past. However, the lack of substantial changes to flood management practices and infrastructure has left Pakistan vulnerable to recurring disasters. As rural communities are displaced by flooding, many are forced to migrate to cities in search of alternative livelihoods. This migration puts additional pressure on already outdated and insufficient urban water infrastructure.

The recurring cycle of water mismanagement and flooding underscores the urgent need for comprehensive reforms in Pakistan's approach to water resource management. From the capital city to the most remote rural areas, the country faces a growing water crisis that demands immediate and effective action. Addressing these challenges will require not only improved infrastructure and management but also a commitment to implementing and enforcing policies that prioritize sustainable water use and flood prevention.

As Pakistan grapples with these interconnected issues, it is clear that the solutions will not be found in quick fixes or superficial measures. Instead, a concerted effort to address the root causes of water scarcity and flooding is needed to build a more resilient and sustainable future for the nation.

Chapter 9: A Canary in Coal Mine?

In a world increasingly aware of the impacts of climate change, countries around the globe face growing challenges related to water scarcity, extreme weather events, and shifting environmental patterns. Pakistan, often cited as a key example of climate vulnerability, has garnered significant attention due to its escalating water crisis. Yet, the crisis in Pakistan offers more than just a warning about climate impacts; it exposes a deeper narrative about political mismanagement and governance failures.

Pakistan's water crisis is a complex phenomenon intertwined with both environmental and political factors. For decades, the country has faced erratic water availability, with some areas experiencing severe droughts while others are inundated with floods.

The Indus River Basin, which serves as the lifeblood of the country, is critically dependent on glacial melting and seasonal rains. Climate change, through altered monsoon patterns, rising temperatures, and accelerated glacial melting, has intensified these challenges, making water management increasingly precarious.

Moreover, the management of meltwater resources is severely hindered due to a lack of availability of adequate data. Meltwater, which is crucial for downstream communities, especially in agriculture and drinking water supply, remains unpredictable because of this scarcity of information.

Bareerah Mirza is a snow data scientist affiliated with Oregon State University, working on the NASA SnowEx project for advancing global snow-water equivalent mapping. She told us, *"The lack of comprehensive snow data and focused research in Pakistan's mountainous regions, particularly in the Himalayas make it increasingly difficult to predict and manage water resources effectively."*

Globally, snow scientists are employing advanced methods like field measurements, modeling, and satellite remote sensing to map snow characteristics such as Snow Water Equivalent (SWE) – a key factor in understanding the water content of snowpacks. *"However, these critical efforts have largely overlooked regions like Pakistan. Inaccessible terrain and the absence of localized studies have introduced uncertainty into models due to unreliable weather data. Without consistent, high-quality information, it is difficult to craft informed water management policies or adequately prepare for potential water shortages that could devastate downstream communities dependent on meltwater,"* Bareerah added.

Climate change is indeed a powerful factor in disrupting weather patterns and rainfall, leading to unpredictable water availability. Shifting monsoon patterns, receding glaciers, rising temperatures, and the increasing frequency of both floods and droughts are all manifestations of this global phenomenon. The Indus River Basin, Pakistan's primary water source, has been severely affected by these changes. **Once abundant with glacial melt and precipitation, the basin has shrunk dramatically, reducing to a mere canal in parts of Sindh Province.** This shrinkage has compelled many farmers to migrate to urban centers, driven by the dire need for water and the loss of arable land.

Pakistan's minimal contribution to global greenhouse gas emissions - less than one percent - exemplifies the disproportionate impact that climate change has on its environment. Despite contributing minimally to global emissions, Pakistan faces severe climate-induced risks, including extreme weather events and significant changes in water availability. This vulnerability underscores the urgent need for both global climate action and effective domestic management.

Yet, with all that is said, it is crucial to recognize that Pakistan's water crisis is not solely a result of environmental factors. Focusing solely on climate change provides an incomplete picture. While global warming undoubtedly influences weather patterns and water availability, Pakistan's water crisis is also a product of ineffective governance, infrastructural decay, and systemic corruption. The country's inability to manage its water resources effectively reflects broader issues within its political and administrative systems.

Attributing Pakistan's water crisis solely to climate change is a misleading oversimplification that masks deeper governance issues. Political leaders frequently invoke climate change to justify their inaction and avoid accountability.

The crisis is deeply rooted in political mismanagement and corruption. Pakistan has sufficient water resources to meet the needs of its population; however, millions of Pakistanis continue to face severe water insecurity.

The country's annual water availability stands at approximately 193 million acre-feet (MAF), significantly exceeding the estimated 7 MAF required for domestic demands.[12] This discrepancy highlights that water scarcity for human use is not because Pakistan is running out of water but due to the mismanagement and unequal distribution of available resources.

The political narrative often shifts the blame to climate change, serving as a convenient excuse to avoid addressing the real issues at hand. This narrative allows political leaders to deflect responsibility and perpetuate a status quo that fails to address the systemic problems within water management. The government's use of climate change as a scapegoat obscures the urgent need for comprehensive political and administrative reforms.

Attributing Pakistan's water crisis solely to climate change is a misleading oversimplification that masks deeper governance issues. Political leaders frequently invoke climate change to justify their inaction and avoid accountability. This approach enables them to sidestep the necessary reforms and maintenance required to manage water resources effectively. The narrative of climate change serves as a smokescreen, concealing the pressing need for political transparency and efficient resource management.

---

[12] Sattar, U. (2023). Pakistan's political economy perpetuates its water crisis. Stimson.

The human factor in the crisis is substantial. The lack of investment in sustainable water infrastructure, coupled with inefficiencies and corruption within existing systems, exacerbates the problem. The government's tendency to blame climate change rather than address these internal issues reflects a broader pattern of neglect and mismanagement.

Pakistan's experience serves as a cautionary tale for other nations facing similar challenges. The interplay between climate change and political mismanagement is a global issue, impacting many countries grappling with environmental and governance issues. The high number of children facing water scarcity in South Asia - 347 million - underscores the severity of the crisis and the need for effective solutions.

The drying up of village wells and the subsequent impacts on homes, health centers, and schools demonstrate the far-reaching consequences of water scarcity. These impacts are not only a result of environmental changes but also reflect the effectiveness of governance structures and political will.

While climate change is a significant factor influencing water crises worldwide, Pakistan's situation illustrates that attributing the crisis solely to environmental factors is a misleading simplification. The country's water woes are deeply intertwined with political mismanagement and corruption.

Addressing the crisis requires a comprehensive approach that considers both climatic impacts and the urgent need for political and administrative reforms. Until these underlying issues are addressed, the water crisis will persist, affecting millions and serving as a stark reminder of the need for effective governance and sustainable resource management.

Chapter 10: Solutions to a Crisis

As we explore solutions to Pakistan's water crisis, it is crucial to recognize that the issue stems more from human management and governance failures than from climate change alone. Addressing this crisis requires a multifaceted approach that prioritizes sustainable and equitable water management practices over costly and debt-inducing mega-infrastructure projects.

Pakistan's water crisis is fundamentally about equity, access, and the fair distribution of resources across various sectors. The focus has long been on building large dams and mega infrastructure projects, neglecting the social and softer aspects of water governance. While India has also prioritized infrastructure development, its greater financial and technical independence has enabled it to mitigate some of the issues faced by Pakistan. For a cash-strapped nation like Pakistan, salvation does not lie in multi-billion dollar projects that further deepen its debt. Instead, more sustainable and cost-effective solutions must be pursued.

One promising solution is the recycling of wastewater. Recall from earlier how Pakistan treats a negligible 1 percent of wastewater.

In contrast, countries like Israel and Singapore have set exemplary standards in this area. Israel, despite being 70% desert, has achieved water security by treating and reusing around 90% of its wastewater, primarily for irrigation. This meets about a quarter of the country's total water demand. Similarly, Singapore meets 40% of its water demand from recycled wastewater, with plans to increase this to 55% by 2060. Adopting such practices can significantly alleviate Pakistan's water scarcity issues by making better use of existing water resources.

Another innovative solution is the concept of **sponge cities**, which has entered 21st-century urban planning and was first pioneered in China.

Despite significant investments in infrastructure, China continued to suffer from urban flooding. The devastating Beijing flood on July 21, 2012, which resulted in 79 deaths, prompted Chinese authorities to embrace the sponge city concept and implement it nationwide. By 2015, China had initiated pilot projects in 16 districts, with plans for 80% of its urban areas to harvest and reuse 70% of rainwater.

Almost a decade later, the results have been promising. Studies indicate that many local pilot initiatives, such as green roofs and rain gardens, have effectively reduced water runoff and mitigated the impacts of flooding.

For example, Wuhan's 389 sponge city projects, covering 38.5 square kilometers, **not only reduced flooding but also sequestered 725 tons of CO_2 annually, lowered temperatures by more than 3°C (5°F), and more than doubled the land value in those areas**.[13]

> The sponge city philosophy aims to distribute and retain water at its source, slow down its flow, clean it naturally, and adapt to it when it accumulates.

[13] Oates, L., Dai, L., Sudmant, A., & Gouldson, A. Building climate resilience and water security in cities: Lessons from the sponge city of Wuhan, China. Coalition for Urban Transitions.

However, the implementation of the sponge city concept has been uneven across China. Although 30 cities were selected as pilot sponge cities in 2015 and 2016, by the following year, only 64 of China's 654 cities had enacted legislation to implement sponge city guidelines. This inconsistency highlights the challenges of scaling such innovative solutions nationwide.

For a sponge city to be successful, it must be tailored to its specific environment, considering factors like topography, rainfall patterns, local flora, and community needs. This tailored approach contrasts with a one-size-fits-all solution, ensuring that the city's unique characteristics are preserved and enhanced.

The success of China's sponge cities has attracted interest from other regions vulnerable to climate change, including Dhaka, Kenya, and major cities like Berlin and Los Angeles. These cities are looking to adopt and implement the sponge city concept in their own urban planning strategies, aiming to mitigate the risks of flooding and other climate-related challenges. As the global climate crisis intensifies, the sponge city model offers a promising avenue for creating resilient and sustainable urban environments.

In Pakistan, cities being unplanned concrete jungles, devoid of vegetation, are leading to frequent flooding. The traditional gray water management model, which focuses on fast discharge, is no longer effective during rapid urbanization. The sponge city philosophy, on the other hand, aims to distribute and retain water at its source, slow down its flow, clean it naturally, and adapt to it when it accumulates. This approach contrasts with conventional solutions that centralize water management through large reservoirs, pipes, and flood walls.

Sponge cities are urban areas designed to absorb rainwater and prevent flooding through the incorporation of natural features such as trees, lakes, and parks. This approach not only reduces flash floods but also improves ecological biodiversity and provides reservoirs for capturing and retaining excess stormwater. Harvested rainwater can be repurposed for irrigation and treated for domestic use if needed. Essentially, it is a form of sustainable urban drainage that enhances a city's resilience to drought.

Natural methods for absorbing urban water are about 50% more affordable than man-made solutions and are 28% more effective, according to research by global design firm Arup and the World Economic Forum. Increasing the "sponginess" of a city can be achieved through stormwater systems, green parks, and well-sized residential gardens. This shift towards green infrastructure is not only a matter of policy change but also a necessity for sustainable urban development.

Implementing sponge city principles in Pakistan can help address both urban flooding and water shortages. By creating more green spaces, wetlands, and permeable pavements, cities can enhance their ability to capture and retain rainwater, thus reducing the risk of floods and conserving water for times of scarcity. Moreover, these measures can improve the overall quality of urban life by providing recreational spaces and enhancing urban biodiversity.

In addition to modern solutions, Pakistan can benefit significantly from reviving ancient water harvesting practices that fell into disuse during British colonial rule. One such practice is the use of stepwells.

For centuries, stepwells, which incorporate a cylindrical well extending down to the water table, provided water for drinking, washing, bathing, and irrigation of crops. These structures were ingeniously designed to provide cleaner water than other sources, such as reservoirs and ponds, by minimizing exposure to sunlight and ensuring a continuous water supply.

Stepwells also served as cool sanctuaries for travelers, caravans, and pilgrims, offering respite from the scorching heat. The temperature at the bottom of these wells was often five to six degrees lower than the surface, providing a natural cooling effect. Evidence of stepwells dates back to the Indus Valley Civilization between 2500-1700 BC. Initially constructed as crude trenches, they evolved into engineering marvels between the 11th and 15th centuries.

Of the thousands of stepwells that existed in what is now Pakistan, most were abandoned in the name of modernization. Neglected, they have silted up, filled with garbage, or crumbled into ruin. Many of these deep wells have turned into dumping yards over the years, with tonnes of debris piling up in them. However, the restoration of these ancient structures can serve a dual purpose of rainwater harvesting and groundwater replenishment. Additionally, they can help avoid urban flooding due to their significant holding capacity.

Restoring stepwells can greatly enhance the self-sufficiency of towns in drought-prone areas, particularly in Sindh. This region, historically dependent on such structures for water, can once again benefit from their use. Moreover, the revival of stepwells has the potential to boost the local economy through tourism. Many restored stepwells have drawn in tourists, creating economic opportunities for local communities.

For instance, the revival of Rani ki Vav in India, a UNESCO World Heritage Site, has attracted tourists from around the world, providing a model for Pakistan. Restoring Pakistan's stepwells can similarly attract tourists, fostering a sense of cultural heritage while addressing water scarcity issues.

Implementing this ancient technology alongside modern solutions like wastewater recycling and sponge cities offers a comprehensive approach to Pakistan's water crisis. By combining the wisdom of the past with contemporary innovations, Pakistan can develop a sustainable and resilient water management system that ensures water security for future generations.

To address the water crisis, increasing agricultural efficiency is crucial. Farmers can adopt precision watering techniques instead of flooding their fields. One of the biggest advances in modern agriculture is drip irrigation, which delivers water directly to the roots of plants, minimizing waste. Additionally, replacing water-intensive crops like sugarcane and rice with lower water-demanding crops can significantly reduce water consumption in agriculture.

Implementing metering for all water users, including domestic, agricultural, and industrial sectors, is essential. Knowing the amount of water utilization enables better planning and management of this precious resource. The current pricing regime offers little incentive for consumers to conserve water. Therefore, linking water pricing to income levels and other dimensions can encourage more judicious use of water. Increasing the cost of water consumption will not only push consumers to use water more efficiently but also generate sufficient revenue for maintaining infrastructure and water-conserving technologies.

Revisiting the colonial Canal and Drainage Act (1873) to equitably tax water usage is another necessary step. Under this act, canal irrigation consumers pay an annual abiana (water tax) charge for water usage. The government charges flat fees ranging from Rs. 400-550 ($2) per acre of farmland for a year of effectively unlimited water use. By comparison, households in Karachi without municipal water supply typically pay more than Rs. 3,300-4,500 ($12-16) for a standard water tanker service every week. Pricing water for nonessential cash crops such as cotton and sugar can help limit potential civil unrest amid growing inflation.

Most importantly, Pakistan must address its political leadership. The political elite, composed largely of feudal landlords, poses the biggest hurdle to necessary reforms. Elite interests tied to water-intensive agriculture have stymied critical changes in the political economy.

In addition, this influence extends to government departments, where the focus shifts away from actual governance and more towards patronage and personal gain.

Departments responsible for flood management and disaster response are particularly affected by this patronage-driven culture, leading to inefficiency and lack of preparedness.

Memon highlights, *"We have response-related institutions, but they lack the necessary resources and authority. While the irrigation department is tasked with flood management, it also plays the role of disaster management, leading to blurred responsibilities and inefficiencies. There is a noticeable gap in performance regarding flood management. Unfortunately, we lack the training capacity and technical expertise needed to handle such disasters effectively, which weakens our response."*

Addressing the water issue would inevitably encounter severe pushback from the political elite because the status quo is critical to their businesses and political stature. Yet, they, too, have to realize that a worsening water crisis ultimately threaten their ability to make any agricultural revenue at all in the years ahead.

Moreover, a state of worsening underdevelopment allows for international aid, which is easier to exploit for rent-seeking than actually improving the country's condition. Foreign aid and loans play a significant role in construction-led development in Pakistan's water sector. While each of these actors secures their own institutional interests, the country's dependency on foreign aid increases, doing little to mitigate the water crisis.

At a local level, communities must be proactive rather than reactive. They should organize towards lasting solutions rather than stop-gap measures. Community-driven initiatives can foster a sense of ownership and responsibility toward water conservation and management, leading to more sustainable outcomes.

Women play an essential role in addressing Pakistan's water crisis, particularly in rural areas where they are often the primary managers of household water. Their involvement in water management is critical to the success of any solution, as they bear the brunt of water scarcity and its consequences.

In many communities, women and girls are responsible for collecting water, a task that can take several hours each day and often involves long distances. This not only affects their health and safety but also limits their opportunities for education and economic activities. By improving water accessibility, we can significantly enhance the quality of life for women and their families.

Empowering women through education and participation in water management decisions can lead to more effective and sustainable solutions. When women are involved in decision-making processes, water projects are more likely to address the specific needs of the community and maintain them over the long term. Training programs that focus on water conservation techniques and efficient usage can also empower women to implement these practices in their households and communities.

Additionally, women have traditional knowledge of local water sources and conservation methods that can be invaluable in developing sustainable water management strategies. Incorporating this knowledge into modern practices can create hybrid solutions that are both effective and culturally acceptable.

Microfinance initiatives aimed at women can also play a significant role in addressing water scarcity. By providing women with the financial resources to invest in water-saving technologies, such as rainwater harvesting systems and drip irrigation, these initiatives can help reduce water wastage and improve agricultural productivity.

By involving women in decision-making processes, providing them with the necessary resources and training, and addressing gender disparities, Pakistan can develop more sustainable and inclusive solutions to its water challenges.

To conclude, Pakistan's water crisis is a complex issue deeply intertwined with political, social, and economic factors. While climate change exacerbates the problem, it is not the sole cause. The crisis is primarily a result of poor governance, inequitable water distribution, and a lack of effective policies. To tackle this issue, Pakistan needs a multifaceted approach that includes modern technological solutions, revival of ancient practices, efficient agricultural methods, equitable water pricing, and, most importantly, political will and community involvement. Only by acknowledging the true nature of the crisis and implementing comprehensive reforms, Pakistan can move towards sustainable water management.

A Closing Thought

In an increasingly interconnected world, it is vital to recognize that the challenges facing any one nation inevitably affect others. Pakistan's current water crisis, exacerbated by climate change, governance shortcomings, and inadequate infrastructure, is no exception. While the primary burden falls on Pakistan, this is not a crisis it can – or should – face alone. Its repercussions will resonate globally, and it is essential to approach the situation with foresight, collaboration, and long-term solutions.

Pakistan's water crisis is multifaceted, touching on climate change, agricultural dependency, and economic vulnerability. Ignoring it could result in severe ripple effects. One immediate concern is the potential for large-scale migration. Climate-induced displacement is a growing global trend, and Pakistan, with its population of over 250 million people, could see a significant wave of refugees seeking better opportunities elsewhere. Rather than dealing with the strain of mass displacement, international support to address the root causes of the crisis now – through financial and technical assistance – would likely be a more effective and humane approach.

Moreover, Pakistan's strategic significance, particularly due to its nuclear arsenal, raises concerns about stability. A failure to address its pressing challenges could lead to insecurity with far-reaching consequences, including risks related to nuclear safety. This is a scenario that demands careful consideration, not alarmism, but steady, coordinated efforts to ensure that such risks are minimized.

We have seen the consequences of state fragility in the past. In the case of Somalia's collapse in the early

1990s, instability spread across the region, impacting global trade and security. Similarly, Libya's descent into chaos following the 2011 uprising led to a proliferation of weapons and militant groups across North Africa and the Sahel, destabilizing neighboring states and exacerbating migration crises in Europe. Syria's protracted civil war not only resulted in a massive humanitarian crisis but also fueled the rise of extremist groups, creating ripple effects on global security and geopolitics.

A similar outcome in Pakistan, which borders key trade routes, could disrupt shipping lanes through piracy and unrest, with potential global economic implications. However, it is important not to oversimplify this issue. Solutions must be nuanced, balancing security concerns with development needs.

The role of the international community, including institutions like the International Monetary Fund (IMF), is crucial here. Pakistan has a history of economic bailouts, but these efforts often focus narrowly on fiscal stability without addressing the deeper, systemic issues. While fiscal discipline is important, conditionalities should not prioritize short-term economic metrics over long-term sustainability. A broader approach is necessary – one that integrates environmental challenges, social equity, and governance reforms alongside economic restructuring.

However, we must be cautious in how we frame the expectations for institutions like the IMF. Traditionally, these organizations focus on economic reforms, and while there is room for more holistic strategies, it is not realistic to expect them to solve all facets of a nation's crisis. This is where international cooperation becomes key. Development aid and loans should encourage reforms that directly tackle Pakistan's water scarcity and climate vulnerability, but they must also respect the complexities of its political and social landscape.

As we look at Pakistan, it is important to remember that this crisis, while severe, is not unique. It is a reflection of the broader challenges that many countries, particularly in the Global South, are starting to face. The international community has an opportunity here – not only to assist Pakistan but also to create a framework for addressing future crises of a similar nature.

In closing, this is a moment for measured, thoughtful action. We cannot afford to wait for the consequences of inaction to unfold. Nor can we rely solely on economic or military solutions to a fundamentally developmental issue. What Pakistan needs is a comprehensive, globally coordinated response that takes into account the full scope of its challenges – environmental, social, and economic. By supporting Pakistan in this way, we not only help one nation, but also strengthen the resilience of our global community in the face of future crises.

Let us proceed with caution but also urgency, and with the understanding that the lessons we learn here can serve as a model for addressing similar challenges in the years ahead.

– A.R. Usmani